The Moral Basis of Fielding's Art

A Study of *Joseph Andrews*

MARTIN C. BATTESTIN

The Moral Basis
of Fielding's Art

A Study of *Joseph Andrews*

Wesleyan University Press
MIDDLETOWN, CONNECTICUT

Copyright © 1959 by Wesleyan University
Library of Congress Catalog Card Number: 59-10177
Manufactured in the United States of America
First edition

for Jeanne

Contents

	Preface	ix
I.	Introduction	3
II.	The Christian Background	14
III.	The Good Man as Hero	26
IV.	Vanity, Fortune, and the Classical Ideal	44
V.	Fielding's Ethics	52
VI.	The Novel: Meaning and Structure	85
VII.	Apology for the Clergy	130
VIII.	Conclusion	150
	Notes	155
	Index	188

Preface

THIS small book grew out of a more ambitious project begun some time ago: namely, the attempt to gather the materials for a badly needed critical, textual, and annotated edition of *Joseph Andrews*. The most elementary question any editor (or any reader, for that matter) must ask himself is finally the most meaningful one: What, after all, is the book about? In this case the pursuit of Fielding's intention led far afield. It was at once apparent that the moral pattern and purpose of *Joseph Andrews* could not be fully understood in isolation from the larger ethical and religious contexts that conditioned them. To establish these contexts and to read the novel as closely as it deserves required more space than an editor's introduction could fairly claim. For this reason, as well as for its relevance to much of Fielding's other work, the subject needed separate treatment.

It will perhaps surprise no one that Fielding undertook this sweeping satire of English society with the Horatian design to instruct as well as to delight his readers, though *Joseph Andrews* is as rich in comedy as any other book in English. It is easy to laugh with Fielding at his Hogarthian gallery of vain and hypocritical innkeepers, squires, justices, parsons, beaus, and coquettes; but, as the theory of the Ridiculous implies, Fielding's laughter is corrective.

A Study of *Joseph Andrews*

He was, as Professor Work observed, a Christian censor of the manners and morals of his age, and of ours as well. The central purposes of this study are to identify the major themes of *Joseph Andrews*, and to view the ethics of the novel in the related contexts of seventeenth- and eighteenth-century latitudinarian Christianity and of Fielding's own morality, which, in its emphasis upon good nature and charity, ultimately derives from such Low Church divines as Isaac Barrow, John Tillotson, Samuel Clarke, and Benjamin Hoadly. There will be time, too, to examine the novel as artifact, and to attempt to satisfy the critics who have looked in vain for a purposeful design in *Joseph Andrews*, for unity and symmetry of structure. Chapter VII discusses an important secondary theme of the novel: Fielding's continuation of the campaign begun in *The Champion* to reform the popular contempt of the clergy.

Although I am convinced, with George Sherburn, that Fielding was "fundamentally a moralist," one thing must be made clear at the start. What is most memorable about Fielding is not his morality or his religion, but his comedy —the warm breath of laughter that animates his fiction. In examining the serious side of Fielding's antic muse, one feels at times uncomfortably like Parson Adams himself, who could declare with typical gravity that there are some things in Steele's *Conscious Lovers* "almost solemn enough for a Sermon" (III, 11).[1] Fielding, we may be sure, knew the difference between comedies and sermons. Any reader of *Joseph Andrews* or *Tom Jones* must agree with the judgment of Coleridge: it is Fielding's cheerful, sunshiny, breezy spirit and the truth and humor of his characters that delight us. But Fielding's mode is satiric; there is bite and purpose in his laughter. Of this modern scholar-

Preface

ship and criticism are well aware. In his own very different way Middleton Murry concurs with Sherburn and Work, and he touches a point pertinent to both the difficulty and the motive of the present study:

The trouble is that Fielding's kind of moral intensity, not being laboured, does not lend itself to laborious analysis and critical expatiation. For that reason it can, apparently, pass entirely unrecognized: dismissed as 'the genial tolerance of the man-about-town', or as 'a simple attitude'. Nevertheless, it exists and is pervasive.[2]

The danger of course remains that, in revealing the moralist in Fielding, we may seem to conceal the satirist. This is the charge that William B. Coley's recent article[3] directs with some justice against a current of modern scholarship of which this book is, all too culpably, a part. While the danger admittedly is real, in this case it would seem inescapable. The job of defining the moral basis of Fielding's art inevitably involves a shift of focus away from comedy. The latitudinarian divines whose wisdom Fielding admired could not match him for wit. It took the lively pen of the novelist to vivify the dusty matter of the homilies. My justification, of course, is the hope that whatever light I may shed on Fielding's meaning and technique will add to the joy of reading him.

Two other things ought to be said about the method of this study. First, I have quoted freely from Fielding and his contemporaries because I feel that wherever possible they should be allowed to speak for themselves, to present the issues that mattered in the language that gives them life better than any paraphrase could do. Second, it will be seen that, like Professor Work, I disagree with those who would explain the relative sobriety of *Amelia, The*

A Study of *Joseph Andrews*

Covent-Garden Journal, and *The Journal of a Voyage to Lisbon* as the result of a sudden "conversion" late in Fielding's career. A shift in tone there may be, but, as the chapter on Fielding's ethics should demonstrate, there is no shift in the essential Christianity of his writings from *The Champion* on. For this reason Chapter V, which discusses Fielding's general moral and religious position by drawing on quotations from works both early and late, also serves as an introduction to the analysis of *Joseph Andrews*.

IT IS A pleasure to thank those to whom I am indebted for advice and assistance in preparing this book. Much of my research was done during my final year in the Graduate School of Princeton University. I am grateful to the Princeton faculty for making that year possible for me by the award of the Peter H. B. Frelinghuysen Fellowship. To every scholar, I suppose, there come those anxious moments when card catalogues refuse to open their secrets. For their kind assistance at such times and for their patient cooperation always, thanks are due to the staffs of the New York Public Library and of the libraries of Princeton, Yale, and Wesleyan universities.

I am especially fortunate to have had as readers of the manuscript those whose knowledge of the eighteenth century and of Fielding is responsible for whatever sanity the book may possess—and, of course, for none of its gaucheries. For their marvelously judicious criticism I am grateful to Professors Louis A. Landa and Henry K. Miller, Jr., of Princeton; Richard L. Greene, of Wesleyan; and George Sherburn, of Harvard. Above all, I wish to thank my friend Professor Landa, who encouraged me in the writing of this book and who generously supervised its progress.

"I, indeed, never read Joseph Andrews."

—DR. JOHNSON

I

Introduction

Henry Fielding wrote his first novel with such good humor and apparent artlessness that his more serious purpose, both as moralist and as craftsman, has been largely overlooked, or at best misapprehended. The old assumptions about the meaning and method of *Joseph Andrews* need to be reappraised. Perhaps the most prevalent and inhibiting supposition about the composition of the novel is the notion that it began simply as another parody of *Pamela* and somehow got gloriously out of hand. When Fielding stumbled upon the irrepressible Parson Adams, we have supposed, he found his true subject and, like Cervantes leading his hero at random from one roadside adventure to another, gave us a very different book from the one he intended. With this as our *donnée*, it is no wonder the novel has seemed formless and disunified. The structure of *Joseph Andrews*, however, including the so-called digression of Mr. Wilson, was quite carefully designed—given substance and shape by Fielding's Christian ethic and by the principle of what he liked to call "that Epic Regularity." From the start the novel had a life and direction of its own.

It is true, of course, that without the fact and fame of *Pamela, Joseph Andrews* would not have been written— not, at least, in just the way it was. Fielding was both

A Study of *Joseph Andrews*

amused and bothered by the astonishing vogue of Richardson's book, which ran through five editions in the eleven months following its initial publication early in November, 1740.[1] If not the "lewd and ungenerous engraftment" that Richardson imagined, *Joseph Andrews* was certainly prompted by the "epidemical Phrenzy" raging over *Pamela*.[2] Indeed, enthusiastic approval of the novel had begun almost immediately. By January, 1741, *The Gentleman's Magazine* observed that it was already *"in Town as great a Sign of Want of Curiosity not to have read* Pamela, *as not to have seen the* French *and* Italian *Dancers."*[3] Later, in the country, the villagers of Slough gathered at the smithy to hear *Pamela* read aloud, and they communally celebrated her marriage by ringing the church bells. "Like the snow, that lay last week, upon the earth and all her products," wrote Aaron Hill to Richardson on December 29, 1740, "[Pamela] covers every other image, with her own unbounded whiteness."[4]

It was this claim—the "whiteness," the moral purity of Richardson's shrewdly chaste young servant maid—that especially irked Fielding. He could scarcely forgive the crass enthusiasm of Dr. Benjamin Slocock, who praised her from the pulpit of St. Saviour's, Southwark.[5] It seemed that even Pope, from whom he might have expected better sense, had been taken in by Pamela's "virtue."[6] To Fielding, London had gone wild over an egregiously bad and pretentious book—a book morally contemptible and technically incompetent. In *The Champion* he had set himself up as Hercules Vinegar, "great champion and censor of Great Britain"—arraigning Colley Cibber, for one, before the bench of the Court of Censorial Inquiry on the charge of murdering the English language;[7] now,

Introduction

as parodist, he would resume his role as arbiter of the good taste of the age.

Early in 1741 Fielding interrupted his labors on behalf of the Patriot opposition to Walpole to write the first, and the best, of the anti-*Pamela*'s. The full title of this brilliant and bawdy parody suggests the line of attack that he hilariously pursues:

> *An Apology for the Life of Mrs. Shamela Andrews. In which, the many notorious Falshoods and Misrepresentations of a Book called* PAMELA, *Are exposed and refuted; and all the matchless Arts of that young Politician, set in a true and just Light. Together with A full Account of all that passed between her and Parson Arthur Williams; whose Character is represented in a manner something different from what he bears in* PAMELA. *The whole being exact Copies of authentick Papers delivered to the Editor. Necessary to be had in all Families. By Mr.* CONNY KEYBER.

Shamela—her pen, even in bed, never out of hand—leads her quarry on, flaunting her charms and "vartue" to catch a squire. By the time the burlesque has run its course, the absurdities and pretensions of *Pamela* have been exposed once and for all. Richardson's vanity in the prefatory "puffs" praising his own performance, the prurience of the bedroom scenes, the clumsiness of the epistolary method, the unconscious hypocrisy of the heroine, and the mercenary morality of "virtue rewarded"—all come, uproariously, under fire.

Critics have long been aware of the significance of *Shamela* as the initial stage in the evolution of *Joseph Andrews*. Besides the apparent ridicule in both books of Richardson's ignorance of life and his art—the blanket criticism of the manners, morality, and method of *Pamela*—similarities in the attacks on the corrupt clergy, on Whitefield and the Methodists, and on Cibber and Conyers Middleton are equally demonstrable. These superficial resemblances, however, have led, curiously, to a general confusion of the very different *motives* that separate a burlesque *jeu d'esprit* from the towering achievement of the epic. The distinction, as we shall see, is Fielding's.

In describing Lady Booby's unsuccessful efforts to seduce her virtuous footman, the opening chapters of *Joseph Andrews* cleverly invert the central situation of *Pamela*. Because of this amusing parallel the assumption has grown that Fielding had again undertaken to parody Richardson until, becoming caught up in the supreme creation of Parson Adams, he by chance evolved the first masterful comic novel in English. One statement of this view, long a critical commonplace, may be taken as typical:

Something very curious seems to have happened. The novel got out of hand, as works of genius sometimes have a way of doing. There is evidence to support this statement in the familiar history of its composition: what began as a travesty of *Pamela* became something very different indeed. Even before the first of the four books comprising the novel was finished, the figure of Parson Adams, who could hardly have been intended to play more than an incidental part in the story of Pamela's chaste brother, entered and swept all before him.[8]

Despite Fielding's clear warning in the Preface to *Joseph Andrews* this misconception began, and has been perpetuated, in a careless failure to distinguish between the modes of parody and satire, or, in his own terms, the *burlesque* and the *comic*. In defining the comic prose epic,

Introduction

Fielding limited the province of his art to the ridiculous (or the comic), deliberately divorcing it from the burlesque, another and inferior kind of ridicule:

Indeed, no two Species of Writing can differ more widely than the Comic and the Burlesque; for as the latter is ever the Exhibition of what is monstrous and unnatural, and where our Delight, if we examine it, arises from the surprising Absurdity, as in appropriating the Manners of the highest to the lowest, or *è converso*; so in the former we should ever confine ourselves strictly to Nature, from the just Imitation of which will flow all the Pleasure we can this way convey to a sensible reader.

Occasional "Parodies or Burlesque Imitations" may be allowed in the comic epic, he remarks, but they must be strictly confined to the *diction*:

In the Diction, I think, Burlesque itself may be sometimes admitted; of which many instances will occur in this Work, as in the Description of the Battles, and some other Places, not necessary to be pointed out to the Classical Reader, for whose Entertainment those Parodies or Burlesque Imitations are chiefly calculated.

But, though we have sometimes admitted this in our Diction, we have carefully excluded it from our Sentiments and Characters; for there it is never properly introduced, unless in writings of the Burlesque kind, which this is not intended to be.

The references here to parody (or burlesque) in *Joseph Andrews* apply strictly, it will be noticed, to the passages in which characteristic epic rhetoric is, by inversion, ludicrously imitated; such, for example, is the humorous comparison of the predatory Mrs. Slipslop to "a hungry Tygress" (I, 6), or the extended mock-heroic description of the battle with the dogs (III, 6).⁹ But even without the statement of the Preface we should not have confused the techniques of the travesty and the novel. The most cursory comparison of *Shamela* and the opening chapters of *Joseph Andrews,* where the recollection of *Pamela* is most vivid, should be proof enough that in the novel Fielding intended something much different—more ambitious, more his own—from what he had attempted in his parody. With one or two deliberate exceptions, such as Joseph's letters to his sister, there is no attempt to mimic the manner and style of Richardson's book. The characteristic Fielding rhetoric is operative from the start.

Fielding well understood the practice and intention of burlesque. He was himself a master of this mode, of which several examples in different genres are *Tom Thumb, The Covent-Garden Tragedy, The Vernoniad, Juvenal's Sixth Satire Modernised in Burlesque Verse,* and, of course, *Shamela. Shamela* is a superb parodic imitation, as Fielding knew it, of *Pamela's* very thought and style. Though the sober Richardson must have winced at its rough and irreverent handling of his materials, Fielding's travesty is really a comic abridgment of its original, even to such a minor feature as the prefatory "puffs." The epistolary manner, the language, the characters, the situations, and (ultimately) the moral of *Pamela* are all retained and imitated so as to reveal their latent absurdities. In *Joseph Andrews,* on the other hand, the resemblances to Richardson's novel are, as it were, *allusive* rather than imitative: such are the initial *donnée* of Lady Booby's attempts on her footman's virtue, Joseph's two letters to his sister, the eventual introduction of Pamela and her squire, and a handful of similar circumstances. Although invariably

Introduction

satiric of *Pamela,* they are meant primarily to *recall* its intellectual and technical inadequacies, while the main narrative of *Joseph Andrews* offers in its place a mature and antithetic alternative—the sweeping social comedy of the epic of the road.

Herein lies the difference. Behind the distinction between the burlesque of *Shamela* and the corrective satire of *Joseph Andrews* are divergent motives. In the first instance Fielding wished to expose the inherent foolishness of Richardson's book. This, he felt, could best be accomplished by the undermining process of parody, the destructive mimicry of the very substance and texture of *Pamela.* But the value of travesty is limited. It is a mode, as J. L. Davis has observed, essentially parasitic, negativistic, and superficial.[10] In *Joseph Andrews* the allusive ridicule of Richardson is intended as a kind of foil, setting off to advantage Fielding's own ambitious attempt at reconstruction, at presenting, in "the Manner of Cervantes," a fresh conception of the art of the novel. This is why the occasional recollection of *Pamela* is most apparent in the early chapters, not because Fielding had exhausted the potential of a nonexistent parody or because he had marvelously stumbled on Parson Adams.[11] The structure of *Joseph Andrews,* despite incidental flaws, is not so haphazard, but rather consciously contrived and symmetrical. Indeed, we might expect no less from a dramatic craftsman and an author who later was capable of writing *Tom Jones.*

By this persistence in a misapprehension of Fielding's intention in his novel, we have been hard pressed to explain the resumed satire of *Pamela.* A little like the fabled spider, we have had to spin out of our imaginations some wonderfully naïve and improbable hypotheses. It has been alleged, for instance, that, disappointed by the failure of *Shamela* to discourage the popularity of Richardson's book, Fielding tried again in *Joseph Andrews*; or that, having originally designed his parody as another assault on Colley Cibber, whom he supposedly thought the author of *Pamela,* he redirected his irony in order to rectify his mistake.[12] But Fielding, who had superbly burlesqued Cibber's "ultra sublime" style in *The Champion* (April 29, May 3, 6, 1740), could scarcely have confused the rhetoric of the *Apology* and *Pamela.* It is doubtful whether such speculation could even plausibly account for a second *Shamela*; it patently fails to explain the achievement of *Joseph Andrews.*

In undertaking his first comic epic in prose, then, Fielding did not mean to subject his rival again to the destructive test of travesty, which he had carried, devastatingly, as far as it would go in *Shamela.* As one anonymous versifier in *The London Magazine* put it, *Shamela* had, once and for all, revealed Richardson's heroine in her true colors — mostly, it would seem, a rather fleshy pink.[13] There was no need to resume the attack with the same weapons. *Joseph Andrews* was written, not in negation of *Pamela,* but in affirmation of a fresh and antithetic theory of the art of the novel. With reference to this art as Fielding conceived it, Richardson's book was above all an example of "the true Ridiculous," as absurd in its own way as the affected and hypocritical justices, clergymen, innkeepers, and fops of society. *Joseph Andrews* was no more designed as a parody of *Pamela* than the sonnets of Donne, let us say, were intended as a burlesque of an effete Petrarchan conventionalism. Fielding recalls his

Introduction

rival not to mimic him as before, but rather to establish a sorry alternative, as it were, a kind of foil to the philosophic and esthetic intuitions that inform his own book from the first sentence to the last. What he offered in return was his own—and, for its time, a highly sophisticated—view of the art of fiction.

But what, precisely, is the moral basis of Fielding's art? Here, largely inspired by James A. Work's essay, "Henry Fielding, Christian Censor,"[14] recent scholarship has achieved some success in clearing away the old clouded notions. Though the arduous job of definition and clarification remains—a task that the present study in part essays—Fielding's ethic has been traced to its source in the popular latitudinarianism of his day. His writings, in fact, furnish such abundant evidence of his sympathies with orthodox Low Church doctrine that it seems odd that we have been so long in uncovering the obvious.

In effect, earlier interpretations implausibly identified Fielding's moral position with that of the caricatured philosopher Square, whose abstract speculations on "the natural beauty of virtue" and "the eternal fitness of things" were, in part at least, "extracted out of the second book of Tully's Tusculan questions, and from the great Lord Shaftesbury."[15] By disregarding contradictory passages, for example, Maria Joesten argued that Fielding's *Weltanschauung* was Stoic: "Sein Weltbild aber ist das stoische, und in der Ethik der Stoa erblickt er die würdigste Norm für das innere Verhalten der freien Persönlichkeit wie für ihr Verhältnis zu der ganzen Menschengemeinschaft."[16] And Aurélien Digeon supposed that Fielding had been a deist before a sobering latter-day "conversion" which vitiated his art in *Amelia*.[17] Expressions of respect for Stoicism are indeed frequent in Fielding's work, and in *Joseph Andrews* a Christianized version of this philosophy underlies much of Parson Adams' moral idealism as well as the hard-earned wisdom of Mr. Wilson. But admiration for the passionless integrity and self-sufficiency of the *vir honestus,* his unfaltering contempt of the vicissitudes of fortune, is almost invariably qualified by an awareness of his limitations. With its stress upon the cultivation of the social affections of benevolence and compassion, its distinctive doctrine of the forgiveness of injuries, and its assurance of the life hereafter, Christianity, said Fielding, "goes much farther."[18]

As for those who inclined to a deistic interpretation of the novels, a majority believed Fielding's emphasis upon natural goodness and social benevolence to be, as Sir John Hawkins had declared with typical impatience, the morality "of lord Shaftesbury vulgarized."[19] Wilbur Cross remarked, for instance, that "in a sober mood [Fielding] would have accepted as completely as did Square the moral doctrines of 'the Great Lord Shaftesbury,'"[20] and George R. Swann similarly believed that Fielding was "greatly influenced" by the author of the *Characteristics.*[21] But, though Fielding occasionally alluded with admiration to Shaftesbury's ingenious essays in literary criticism, *Soliloquy; or Advice to an Author* and *Sensus Communis; An Essay on the Freedom of Wit and Humour,*[22] he generally avoided recommendation of the ethical views of the *Characteristics.* Many aspects of Shaftesbury's thought undoubtedly appealed to him—the belief, for example, in an innate moral sense and in the naturalness of the social affections—but these, as R. S. Crane has shown, were ideas that Shaftesbury held in common with the latitudinarians.[23]

Introduction

Fielding, moreover, unquestionably disliked the deistic principles of the *Characteristics*. The inadequacy of Square's speculative Shaftesburianism is clearly demonstrated by its inability to account for the reality of unmerited suffering (the occasion of Tom's broken arm) or to provide a reliable moral imperative (the encounter in Molly Seagrim's closet). In Square's eventual acceptance of Christian revelation we may witness the ultimate insufficiency of a philosophy founded solely upon the cant concepts of "the natural beauty of virtue" and "the eternal fitness of things." Indeed, as early as *The Champion* (January 22, 1739/40) and *Joseph Andrews* (III, 3), Fielding implicitly criticized Shaftesburian tendencies along with those "political philosophers" who denied the immortality of the soul and the personal providence of God, and who, like the members of Mr. Wilson's freethinking club, professed to replace Christian incentives to virtue with "the infallible Guide of Human Reason" and the "Rule of Right."

It is the liberal moralism of the Low Church divines —not the principles of Cicero or Shaftesbury—that underlies the ethos, and much of the art, of *Joseph Andrews*.

II

The Christian Background

THE MODIFIED Pelagian doctrine of such latitudinarian churchmen as Isaac Barrow, John Tillotson, Samuel Clarke, and Benjamin Hoadly—all of whom Fielding read with sympathy and admiration[1]—is essential background for a right interpretation of his ethics in general and of the meaning of *Joseph Andrews* in particular. In the sermons of these divines and others who shared their belief in a pragmatic, common-sense Christianity, he found ready made a congenial philosophy of morals and religion. It was an optimistic philosophy stressing the perfectibility, if not the perfection, of the human soul, and one directed toward the amelioration of society. In both respects it was exactly suited to the satirist's purposes. We may look here for the sources of Fielding's didacticism, for the rationale behind the ethic of good nature and good works that distinguishes his writing from *The Champion* to the end of his career.

The early latitudinarians were prominent in the late seventeenth-century reaction against the cynical moral relativism of Hobbes, the strict rationalism of the neo-Stoics, and the Antinomian tendencies of Calvinism. Developing an optimistic (though unorthodox) interpretation of human nature, they formulated, in effect, a religion of practical morality by which a sincere man might earn

The Christian Background

his salvation through the exercise of benevolence. Against the author of the *Leviathan,* for example, Tillotson defended the naturalness of the benevolent social affections: "So far is it from being true, which Mr. Hobbes asserts as the fundamental principle of his politics, 'That men are naturally in a state of war and enmity with one another' ..."[2] And because they placed so much emphasis upon the tender passions that motivate charitable actions, the divines criticized the Stoic ideal of insensitive detachment as both reprehensible—"a mark of the greatest degeneracy and depravation of human nature"[3]—and unrealistic—"so extravagant and unpracticable, because they framed them not according to the real nature of man, such as is existent in the world, but according to an idea formed in their own imaginations."[4] Within the Church, the latitudinarians, though never expressly admitting to it, were engaged in promulgating an extreme form of Arminianism, which after 1720 became scarcely distinguishable from Socinianism or Pelagianism, "the classic example of a Christianity stressing God too little and Man too much."[5] In their insistence on natural depravity (IX), justification by faith only (XI), the insufficiency of good works (XII-XIII), and predestination (XVII), the Articles of the Church were rooted in the tradition of Augustine and Calvin. But this orthodoxy was now giving way before a complacent moralism that made salvation universal and largely dependent upon the condition of an active, comprehensive charity.

Basic to the latitudinarian position was a belief in the essential goodness of human nature. Although the divines might acknowledge man's weakness since the Fall and admit the requirement of faith, yet these concessions to orthodoxy were merely perfunctory. The recurrent drift of their writing was the naturalness of the social affections and man's capacity for moral perfection. Human nature, they repeatedly affirmed, was inherently noble, but corrupted through bad education and custom. Thus Isaac Barrow could ask:

Is there not to all men in some measure, to some men in a higher degree, a generosity innate, most lovely and laudable to all; which disposeth men with their own pain, hazard, and detriment to succour and relieve others in distress, to serve the public, and promote the benefit of society; so that inordinately to regard private interest doth thwart the reason and wisdom of nature?[6]

In a passage that may have inspired Dr. Harrison's defense of human nature in *Amelia* (IX, 5) Barrow became more definite: "There do remain, dispersed in the soil of human nature, divers seeds of goodness, of benignity, of ingenuity, which being cherished, excited, and quickened by good culture, do, to common experience, thrust out flowers very lovely, yield fruits very pleasant of virtue and goodness." Man, "if well managed, if instructed by good discipline, if guided by good example, if living under the influence of wise laws and virtuous governors," is naturally inclined to benevolence; however, "from neglect of good education; from ill conduct, ill custom, ill example," wickedness and folly are rife.[7]

Similarly, Tillotson was convinced that "nothing is more unnatural than sin; 'tis not according to our original nature and frame, but it is the corruption and depravation of it, a second nature superinduced upon us by custom."[8] And Samuel Clarke echoed his predecessors in declaring

The Christian Background

that compassion, the seed of benevolence, is "implanted in the very frame of our Nature; and men cannot without great and long habits of Wickedness, root out of their minds so noble and excellent an inclination."[9] This constant emphasis upon the human potential for perfection, if only the corrosive pressures of corrupted custom, education, and example could be removed, afforded a convenient rationale for Fielding's social satire.

In one important respect especially, these clergymen differed from Shaftesbury, whose views of human nature they anticipated. By making an active charity the condition of salvation, they realistically implemented their exhortations to cultivate the benevolent affections. Though common to all men, good nature, as Barrow carefully noticed, was given "to some in a higher degree." Against the deists, who frequently asserted that the natural beauty of virtue and the reason of things were sufficient incentives to moral action, Samuel Clarke objected that such arguments were feasible only "in their proper place and season, to generous and considerate minds, and in suitable Circumstances of things."[10] But in a world confused and corrupted through weakness and ill custom, the stronger inducements of future rewards and punishments were required.

Good nature, or rather its specific manifestation in a comprehensive and energetic charity, became the core of latitudinarian Christianity, which had as its goal the practical betterment of society no less than the salvation of individual souls. The Golden Rule was the sum and "the Practice of *Virtue*" the end of religion.[11] Writing in 1702, Hoadly thus succinctly described his position: "Did Men but consider, that the great Branch of Christian Duty, is

A Study of *Joseph Andrews*

Love, and Good-nature, and Humanity; and the distinguishing Mark of a *Christian*, an universal Charity; they could not but own that *Jesus Christ* came to plant and propagate them in the World."[12] On the bitterly debated question of the relative importance of faith or works, these rational divines stood staunchly with St. James against St. Paul; "Faith without works is dead" was a text repeated in countless sermons. "The great and solemn Audit to come," declared Hoadly in a sermon that Fielding evidently reflected in *Joseph Andrews*, "turns all upon Charity."[13] What the latitudinarians meant by charity, however, was not mere alms-giving, but an active, universal love of humanity, embracing friend and enemy, expressed by practice and not merely by profession, and limited only by the opportunity and power of the individual. In Isaac Barrow's sermon, "The Duty and Reward of Bounty to the Poor," one of Fielding's particular favorites and important to an understanding of the ethos of his first novel, charity is made the essential characteristic of the good man. More than a simple liberality, it is rather a consuming, comprehensive virtue, touching the individual's every dealing with his neighbor, implying

> ... a kind of universality in the matter of his beneficence; that he bestoweth whatever he hath within compass of his possession, or his power.... Every thing, I say, which he hath in substance, or can do by his endeavour, that may conduce to the support of the life, or the health, or the welfare in any kind of his neighbour, to the succour or relief of his indigency, to the removal or easement of his affliction, he may well here be understood to disperse and give. Feeding the hungry, clothing the naked, visiting the sick, entertaining the stranger, ransoming the captive, easing the oppressed, comforting the

The Christian Background

sorrowful, assisting the weak, instructing or advising the ignorant, together with all such kinds or instances of beneficence, may be conceived . . . as the matter of the good man's dispersing and giving.[14]

Rooted in a good-natured, disinterested compassion, this selfless benevolence was sharply distinguished from the stinted, politic charity of the Hobbes-Mandeville conception, against which Barrow exclaimed, "All their shows of friendship and respect are mercenary, and mere trade; they do nothing *gratis,* or for love."[15] Similarly, Tillotson declared the worthlessness and hypocrisy of charity done from motives other than "an inward principle of love to God and goodness"; if we are selfishly virtuous "only to serve our temporal interest, though the actions we do be never so good, yet all the virtue and reward of them is lost, by the mean end and design which we aim at in the doing of them."[16] Indeed, as the "great source of uncharitableness" and "the great root of all the disorders and mischiefs in the world,"[17] self-love in its various forms detrimental to society—avarice, ambition, vanity, hypocrisy—was the object of the divines' sharpest censure. In passages quite close to Fielding's criticism of the lawyer (III, 1) and to Mr. Wilson's fulmination against vanity as the chief vice (III, 3), Barrow condemned that moral solipsism that makes self the sole center of creation:

> We would be the only men, or most considerable, in the world; hence are we ambitious, hence continually with unsatiable greediness we do affect and strive to procure increase of reputation, of power, of dignity.
> We would engross to ourselves all sorts of good things in highest degree; hence enviously we become jealous of the worth

and virtue, we grudge and repine at the prosperity of others; as if they defalked somewhat from our excellency, or did eclipse the brightness of our fortune.[18]

Charity, then, in the exalted sense of a disinterested, active, and universal benevolence, was the sum of religion and the indispensable duty of every Christian. Faith, knowledge, and ritual without it were mere Pharisaism, dead and perfunctory. For Barrow, true religion consisted "not in a nice orthodoxy" but "in an inward good complexion of mind, exerting itself in works of true devotion and charity"[19]—a sentiment that virtually epitomized the latitudinarian position and that was reiterated, in slightly different words, in scores of sermons, not the least of which was Hoadly's influential discourse on "The Nature of the Kingdom, or Church, of Christ." It informs as well Hoadly's rational, mystery-dispelling interpretation of the eucharist in *A Plain Account of the Nature and End of the Sacrament of the Lord's Supper,* which Parson Adams praises extravagantly (I, 17). To Hoadly, the sacrament was instituted as a simple outward memorial of Christ's sacrifice, the observance of which alone could not merit that salvation that belonged "only to the whole System of *Christian Practice.*"[20] For these Christian divines, faith and knowledge were significant solely as moral virtues productive of charity. "A right faith is wholly in order to a good life, and is of no value any farther than it hath an influence upon it," declared Tillotson. "The knowledge of religion is only in order to the practice of it; and an article or proposition of faith is an idle thing, if it do not produce such actions as the belief of such a proposition doth require."[21] The contention that salvation was "*not* according

The Christian Background

to mens *Faith* or *Knowledge,* if they be void of the Fruits of Righteousness" was, indeed, fundamental to this religion of social morality.[22] Men were to be judged not according to their credulity or professions, but according to the demonstrated goodness of their lives. For a reason we need go no farther than Addison's observation that, with respect to society, "infidelity is not of so malignant a nature as immorality."[23]

In one respect at least, this Pelagian doctrine corresponded to the deism, for example, of Lord Herbert of Cherbury, who had refused to believe that a benevolent God would condemn those ignorant of scriptural revelation. With sincerity and charity as their principal criteria, the latitudinarians professed greater hopes for the virtuous heathen, acting under the dictates of Reason and the Law of Nature, than for the vicious believer in Christ. This position was asserted on several occasions by Barrow, Clarke, and Tillotson, all of whom agreed generally with the Archbishop's pronouncement:

I know no such error and heresy as a wicked life. That man believes the gospel best, who lives most according to it. . . . I had rather a man should deny the satisfaction of Christ, than believe it, and abuse it to the encouragement of sin. Of the two, I have more hopes of him that denies the divinity of Christ, and lives otherwise soberly, and righteously, and godly in the world, than of the man who owns Christ to be the Son of God, and lives like a child of the devil.

Such a faith as hath not an answerable life will be ineffectual to the purpose of justification and salvation.[24]

Indeed, this part of latitudinarian doctrine was so familiar that Addison, in *The Spectator,* No. 459, could note as "generally owned" that "there may be salvation for a virtuous infidel (particularly in the case of invincible ignorance), but none for a vicious believer."[25] In particular, however, Hoadly's phrasing of this commonplace is memorable for its unusual closeness to Parson Adams' own opinion: "We may be . . . certain, That an honest *Heathen* is much more acceptable to [God], than a dishonest and deceitful *Christian*; and that a charitable and good-natured *Pagan* has a better Title to his Favour, than a cruel and barbarous Christian; let him be never so orthodox in his Faith."[26]

Within the Church the special antagonism of the rationalistic divines was reserved for Antinomianism, the doctrine of unconditional justification by faith and the imputed righteousness of Christ without regard to works. Tillotson inveighed against the danger to society latent in a theory that removed the religious sanctions to morality and cleared the way to licentiousness: ". . . those luscious doctrines of the Antinomians, concerning free grace, and the justification of a sinner merely upon a confident persuasion of his being in a state of grace and favour with God, and consequently that the gospel dischargeth men from obedience to the laws of God, and all manner of obligation to the virtues of a good life."[27] And Robert South, whose witty sermons Fielding loved to read, deplored "that doctrine that holds that the covenant of grace is not established upon conditions, and that nothing of performance is required on man's part to give him an interest in it, but only to believe that he is justified; this certainly subverts all the motives of a good life."[28]

By 1739 the strongly Calvinistic preaching of the great evangelist, George Whitefield, who with John Wesley was

The Christian Background

inaugurating the Methodist revival, had caused the violent resumption of the Antinomian controversy. Although of the moralists we have been considering Hoadly alone remained to witness the Great Awakening, their successors brought the old arguments to bear against this new and formidable adversary. The distinctive tenets of the fiery Methodist—though really in close agreement with the Calvinistic Articles of the Church—naturally came into conflict with the rational, Pelagian morality of the latitudinarians. His insistence, for example, upon spiritual regeneration through the sensible influx of God's grace was decried as "madness and enthusiasm" by those who followed Locke in stressing the reasonableness of Christianity; to Tindal, Hogarth, Smollett, Dr. Johnson, and others, such pretensions to divine afflatus were at best fanaticism, at worst hypocrisy.[29]

Especially repugnant, however, were Whitefield's views of justification by faith alone. A thorough Calvinist, he insisted in 1740 on the utter depravity of the natural man unregenerated by grace. Salvation was not to be earned by mere moral performances:

What think you then, if I tell you, that you are to be justified freely through faith in Jesus Christ, without any regard to any work or fitness foreseen in us at all? For salvation is the free gift of God. I know no fitness in man, but a fitness to be cast into the lake of fire and brimstone for ever. Our righteousnesses in God's sight, are but as filthy rags: he cannot away with them.[30]

Earlier, in 1739, he had admonished his followers "to contend earnestly for the doctrine of *Justification by faith only*":

The lively oracles no where declare good works to be a necessary condition of our justification in the sight of God. . . .

We must not expect to be saved, or any way recommend ourselves to God, by any or all the works of righteousness which we have done, or shall, or can do. The Lord Christ is our righteousness,—our whole righteousness: imputed to us, instead of our own. . . . [And, after citing Article XI in his support] Christ, by his sacrifice, and perfect obedience, has every way fulfilled the law for us; and God will not require to be paid twice. Christ bought our justification with a great price, even with his own blood. It comes to us freely, without any regard to works past, present, or to come.[31]

To Whitefield, the works doctrine of the latitudinarians —he was especially severe with Tillotson and the author of *The Whole Duty of Man*—was a travesty of Christianity. He was irritated by their exaltation of the "honest moral man" who, to merit salvation, merely "does justly, and, what the world calls, loves a little mercy, is now and then good-natured, reacheth out his hand to the poor, receives the sacrament once or twice a year, and is outwardly sober and honest."[32] By emphasizing good nature and social benevolence, the established clergy, he felt, were supplying their flocks "only with the dry husks of dead morality":[33]

My dear brethren, *Seneca, Cicero, Plato,* or any of the heathen philosophers, would have given as good a definition as this: It means no more, than reflecting that we have done well. This, this is only Deism refined.[34]

Although there was much truth in this criticism, Whitefield's opponents, with equal justice, charged that the "licentious doctrine" of faith and grace made salvation

The Christian Background

too comfortably a matter of personal confidence rather than active demonstration; such a belief was too open to hypocrisy and dangerously subversive of the highest sanctions of social morality. Virtually repeated by Parson Adams (I, 17), the popular, though mistaken, rendering of Whitefield's position was, "So you say you believe in the Lord Jesus Christ, you may live the life of devils."[35] It was a doctrine inevitably distasteful to a practical Christianity that preached the good life of social benevolence as the end of religion.

III

The Good Man as Hero

Joseph Andrews was affected in various and surprising ways — structurally as well as thematically — by the writings of the moralists. Emerging from the benevolist ethic and its insistence upon the need for appropriate *exempla* as the best inspiration to the good life, a concept of the moral man as hero took shape in the homiletic literature of the period, and it is of considerable importance to an understanding of Joseph Andrews and Abraham Adams, "valuable Patterns"—as Fielding called them, with less tongue in cheek than we might suppose—of chastity and charity. The true origin of Fielding's twin protagonists in their capacity as moral exemplars in this low-life epic of the road may be traced with confidence to the homilies, and in particular, it would seem, to Isaac Barrow's sermon "Of Being Imitators of Christ." The sermons present four points of special significance: (1) the depiction of the good man as hero; (2) the notion that the sum of his goodness is *chastity* (or virtue or temperance, the control of reason over the passions) with respect to himself, and *charity* with respect to society; (3) the choice of Joseph and his rejection of Potiphar's wife to exemplify the former, and of the pilgrim patriarch Abraham, the epitome of human faith expressed in works, to represent the latter; and (4) the analogy of the good man's life

The Good Man as Hero

in a world of vanity and vexation to a pilgrimage through strange lands to his true home.

Widely prevalent in the writings of the moralists, the exaltation of the good man was the natural corollary of the importance that the latitudinarians attached to good nature and charity. Greatness, or superiority in worldly power, wealth, and honor, was contemned (in theory at least) as ethically inferior to goodness. From this effort to shift esteem from the achievements of the selfish passions to the exercise of temperance and benevolence, the moral man emerged as hero. Making an active philanthropy the essential characteristic of the good man, Isaac Barrow, in a passage apparently echoed by Joseph Andrews (III, 6), insisted that charity is the only source of true honor: "All good actions as such are honourable: but of all virtues, beneficence doth with most unquestionable right claim honour, and with irresistible force procures it; as it is indeed the most divine of virtues, so men are most apt to venerate them, whom they observe eminently to practise it."[1] Samuel Clarke, however, perfectly summarized the concept:

> There is nothing in nature more amiable, than the character of a truly *Good* man; a Man, whose principal Business and Pleasure is to make all Men easy, with whom he has any Concern, in the *present* life; and to promote, as far as in Him lies, their Happiness likewise in That which is *to come*. *Other* Qualifications, have their *Value*; and do in their proportion, merit a just degree of Esteem. Great Knowledge and Abilities, every where necessarily command Respect. Great Actions never fail to fill Men with Admiration, and to procure Applause. But of *all* Characters, That of *Goodness* is the most *lovely*; and approaches nearest to the Similitude of a *Divine* Perfection.[2]

A Study of *Joseph Andrews*

Eulogies of this new hero, whose pattern for emulation was frequently Christ or Abraham or the Good Samaritan, abound in the homilies. Besides those already adduced, portraits of the good man may be drawn from Barrow's "Of Walking As Christ Did," "Of the Love of Our Neighbour," and "Of Being Imitators of Christ"; from Clarke's "Of Believing in God" and, especially, "The Character of a Good Man"; from Tillotson's "The Example of Jesus in Doing Good" and "Good Men Strangers and Sojourners upon Earth"; and from Hoadly's sermon on "St. Paul's Discourse to Felix" and "The Good Samaritan."

But the superiority of the moral man's spiritual heroism when compared with the worldly greatness of the statesman and warrior is illustrated most extensively in Richard Steele's *The Christian Hero: An Argument Proving that No Principles but Those of Religion are Sufficient to Make a Great Man* (1701). In accord with the moralizing divines, Steele stressed the supremacy of Christian humility, forgiveness, and charity—"the neglected and despised Tenets of Religion ... so Generous, and in so Transcendent and Heroick a manner disposed for publick Good"[3]—over the imperfect and self-centered Stoic virtues; and to the examples of Caesar, Cato, and Brutus he contrasted the higher heroism of Christ and the Apostles, "Characters the most truly Gallant and Heroick that ever appear'd to Mankind."[4] In *The Spectator*, No. 248, it is Steele again who defines the nature of true greatness and heroism as the exercise of benevolence, which may be found in even the lowest levels of society:

> THERE are none who deserve superiority over others in the esteem of mankind, who do not make it their endeavour to

The Good Man as Hero

be beneficial to society; and who, upon all occasions which their circumstances of life can administer, do not take a certain unfeigned pleasure in conferring benefits of one kind or other. . . . Where opportunities and inclinations are given to the same person, we sometimes see sublime instances of virtue, which so dazzle our imaginations that we look with scorn on all which in lower scenes of life we may ourselves be able to practise. But this is a vicious way of thinking; and it bears some spice of romantic madness for a man to imagine that he must grow ambitious, or seek adventures, to be able to do great actions. It is in every man's power in the world, who is above mere poverty, not only to do things worthy but heroic. The great foundation of civil virtue is self-denial; and there is no one above the necessities of life but has opportunities of exercising that noble quality, and doing as much as his circumstances will bear for the ease and convenience of other men; and he who does more than ordinarily men practise upon such occasions as occur in his life, deserves the value of his friends as if he had done enterprises which are usually attended with the highest glory. Men of public spirit differ rather in their circumstances than their virtue; and the man who does all he can in a low station is more an hero than he who omits any worthy action he is able to accomplish in a great one.[5]

The notion of the Christian hero, thus recommended by both Steele and the homilists, enjoyed an unusual popularity during the first half of the century, even becoming the subject of a poetry contest conducted by *The Gentleman's Magazine*.[6]

Underlying many of the most memorable characters in eighteenth-century literature—Sir Roger de Coverly, Squire Allworthy, Dr. Harrison, Sir Charles Grandison, Dr. Primrose, Uncle Toby, and, of course, Parson Adams— the theory of the good man reduced his essential characteristics to two: personal chastity (representative of the temperate discipline of the passions) and social charity. Thus Tillotson offered as the two comprehensive rules of morality:

> ... that we govern our passions by reason, and moderate our selves in the use of sensual delights, so as not to transgress the rules of temperance and chastity; that we demean our selves towards others, and converse with them with justice and fidelity, with kindness and charity.
>
> These are the sum of the divine laws, and the heads of our duty towards our selves and others.[7]

Bishop Hoadly, who regretted the degeneration of Christianity since the time of St. James, even more succinctly summed up true religion as "Virtue and Integrity, as to Ourselves, and Charity and Beneficence to Others."[8]

Of particular significance for *Joseph Andrews*, however, is the choice of Joseph and Abraham, respectively, as *exempla* of these comprehensive virtues. As the supreme illustration (after St. James II: 20-24) of faith perfected and expressed through works, Abraham in the homilies became synonymous with the good man. In "The Duty and Reward of Bounty to the Poor," for example, Barrow cites the patriarch as the highest example of the good man, whose chief characteristic is charity:

> Also in the particular histories of good men, this sort of practice [i.e., charity] is especially taken notice of, and expressed in their characters. In the story of our father Abraham, his benignity to strangers, and hospitableness, is remarkable among all his deeds of goodness, being propounded to us as a pattern and encouragement to the like practice.

The Good Man as Hero

Alluding to Luke XIX: 8-9, Barrow then recalls Christ's declaration that a charitable man is *"a son of Abraham."*[9] In "The Love of Our Neighbour," the patriarch's voluntary pilgrimage is remembered as a model of selfless benevolence in action: "Did not Abraham even prefer the good of others before his own, when he gladly did quit his country, patrimony, friends, and kindred, to pass his days in a wandering pilgrimage . . . ?"[10] Tillotson similarly identifies him with the good man.[11] Samuel Clarke's "The Character of a Good Man" presents Abraham as its chief pattern for his "adhering stedfastly to the *True Religion*, in the *midst* of idolatrous and corrupt Nations."[12] In "Of Believing in God" he is styled "the great Example of Righteousness," whose faith was true because productive of works. Clarke thus explains the choice of Abraham as the type of true piety:

Herein consisteth the Faith of *Abraham*; that, in the midst of an idolatrous World, he constantly retained this Notion of the One invisible God of the whole Universe; and trusted in him, and served him, and obeyed him accordingly, in all Holiness and Righteousness of Life; depending upon a remote and invisible Reward; and therefore he was styled, the *Friend* of God, and was set forth as a perpetual Example of True Faith to all succeeding generations.[13]

Because they stressed an active faith and charity, the churchmen thus established Abraham, with particular emphasis upon his pilgrimage through strange and idolatrous lands, as the type of complete human goodness.

As exemplifying the more personal virtue of chastity, Joseph's withstanding the blandishments of Potiphar's wife was equally familiar. Barrow's "Of the Virtue and

A Study of *Joseph Andrews*

Reasonableness of Faith" and South's "Deliverance from Temptation the Privilege of the Righteous" both recall the story as an instance of moral integrity resisting temptation.[14] But here there is really no need to multiply citations. The continence of Joseph had long been proverbial, the standard biblical prototype of male chastity—and a favorite, we might add, with Fielding.[15] Joseph Andrews himself called attention to the analogy between his own situation and that of "Joseph my namesake" (I, 10), and earlier in the novel Fielding pointedly noticed the chastity of his hero, "whom, for a good Reason, we shall hereafter call JOSEPH" (I, 5).

Although efforts have been made to explain the naming of Fielding's characters on other, less calculated grounds,[16] the names of the heroes of his first novel were selected for reasons, Andrews being the surname of Richardson's heroine and Adams appropriately suggestive of the natural innocence and good nature of the parson. From our investigation of the homilies and the theory of the good man, it would seem that their Christian names were quite deliberately chosen.

The image of the good man as hero, with Abraham and Joseph as exemplars of his essential virtues, was thus a commonplace well before *Joseph Andrews* was begun. But for the crystallization of the concept and for an explanation of its didactic function within the genre of history,[17] Fielding seems to have been particularly indebted to the sermon "Of Being Imitators of Christ," by his "favourite" divine, Isaac Barrow. Briefly, the subject of Barrow's discourse is the duty of imitating the examples of good men, with emphasis on the special efficacy of history in promoting this end and on the superiority of

The Good Man as Hero

the Old Testament heroes to the classical as moral patterns.

Before looking at Barrow's sermon more closely, however, we may profitably recall the opening paragraphs of *Joseph Andrews,* in which Fielding, like Barrow, proposes the usefulness of the good man's example as prompting to imitation, and declares the moral function of the historian to be the communication of "such valuable Patterns" to the world:

> It is a trite but true Observation, that Examples work more forcibly on the Mind than Precepts: and if this be just in what is odious and blameable, it is more strongly so in what is amiable and praiseworthy. Here Emulation most effectually operates upon us, and inspires our Imitation in an irresistible manner. A good Man therefore is a standing Lesson to all his Acquaintance, and of far greater use in that narrow Circle than a good Book.
>
> But as it often happens that the best Men are but little known, and consequently cannot extend the Usefulness of their Examples a great Way; the Writer may be called in aid to spread their History farther, to present the amiable Pictures to those who have not the Happiness of knowing the Originals; and by communicating such valuable Patterns to the World, may perhaps do a more extensive Service to Mankind than the Person whose Life originally afforded the Pattern.

As the ethical antithesis to the vanity and hypocrisy of society, the four books of Fielding's first novel present the examples of two such good men named Joseph and Abraham.

The direct influence of Barrow's sermon upon the conception of *Joseph Andrews* may be proposed with reasonable assurance. Asserting the peculiar effectiveness of history in promoting morality, for instance, Barrow anticipates Fielding's introduction: "Examples do more compendiously, easily, and pleasantly inform our minds, and direct our practice, than precepts, or any other way or instrument of discipline." And he adds later, quoting Juvenal, "As . . . it is a great blemish and reproach to human nature that, *We*, as the Satirist truly observeth of us, *have a great proclivity to follow naughty examples*; so there is from hence some amends, that we have also some inclination to imitate good and worthy precedents; the which is somewhat more strong and vigorous, because countenanced and encouraged by the approbation of reason, our most noble faculty."[18] Developing an old idea, he then explains at some length the didactic superiority of example to precept, the former being "the most facile, familiar, and delightful way of instruction," in which, "like a picture . . . you see at once described the thing done, the quality of the actor, the manner of doing, the minute seasons, measures, and adjuncts of the action."[19] The careers of the patriarchs in "the divine histories," Barrow says, were designed that we might "imitate those illustrious patterns of virtue and piety,"[20] and they are especially adaptable to that purpose since "one good example may represent more fully and clearly to us the nature of a virtue, than any verbose description thereof can do."[21]

Most interesting with regard to *Joseph Andrews* is Barrow's choice of *exempla*. His good men are (1) Abraham, illustrative of true faith, and (2) Joseph, the pattern of chastity. When read with the heroes and action of *Joseph Andrews* in mind, Barrow's accounts of the careers of these biblical heroes are striking:

The Good Man as Hero

For instance, if we desire to know what faith is . . . let us propose to our consideration the practice of Abraham; wherein we may see the father of the faithful leaving a most pleasant country, the place of his nativity, and questionless most dear unto him under that notion; deserting his home and fixed habitation, his estate and patrimony, his kindred and acquaintance, to wander he knew not where in unknown lands . . . leading an uncertain and ambulatory life in tents, sojourning and shifting among strange people, devoid of piety and civility, (among Canaanites and Egyptians,) . . .[22]

Though they are not, of course, Canaanites and Egyptians whom Adams meets in his travels, so many deeds of uncharitableness as he encounters along the highway remind the parson of their eighteenth-century counterparts: "he almost began to suspect that he was sojourning in a Country inhabited only by Jews and Turks" (II, 16). Barrow's description of Joseph's withstanding the temptation of Potiphar's wife might stand as an abridged version of the first ten chapters of the novel:

Again, he that would learn how to demean himself in resisting the assaults of temptation, let him perpend that one carriage of Joseph; of him, together withstanding the courtships of an attractive beauty, and rejecting the solicitations of an imperious mistress, advantaged by opportunities of privacy and solitude; when the refusal was attended with extreme danger, and all the mischiefs, which the disdain of a furious lust disappointed, of an outrageous jealousy provoked . . . could produce; and all this by one of meanest condition, in a strange place, where no intercession, favour, or patronage of friends could be had, no equal examination of his cause might be expected; of him doing this, merely upon principles of conscience, and out of fear of God . . . and he that considers this example, how can he be ignorant of his duty in the like case?[23]

A Study of *Joseph Andrews*

If, as he began to write *Joseph Andrews,* Fielding did have in mind Barrow's treatment of the function of history in communicating patterns of goodness—and the points of similarity in content and organization seem too close to be coincidental—he would have found in this same discourse further justification, on ethical grounds, of his own favorite genre. To Barrow, history pre-eminently combined delight with instruction to the great end of morality: "No kind of studious entertainment doth so generally delight as history, or the tradition of remarkable examples." Even the most apathetic students warm to "historical narrations; these striking them with a delectable variety of accidents, with circumstantial descriptions, and sensible representations of objects, do greatly affect and delight their fancies; especially the relation of notable adventures and rare accidents is wont to be attended with great pleasure and satisfaction."[24] Again, relevant to the character and function of Parson Adams, Fielding's mock-heroic patriarch and priest, Barrow preferred the biblical accounts of "the lives and examples of holy men" to those relating "the most famous achievements of Pagan heroes." Here Abraham, in his martial capacity, is said to surpass Alexander. The comparison continues:

No triumphs indeed are comparable to those of piety; no trophies are so magnificent and durable, as those which victorious faith erecteth: that history therefore which reports the *Res gestae,* the acts and sufferings of most pious men, must in reason be esteemed not only the most useful, but also the most pleasant; yielding the sweetest entertainment to well-disposed minds; wherein we see virtue expressed, not in bare idea only, but in actual life, strength, motion; in all its beauty and ornaments: than which no spectacle can be more stately; no

The Good Man as Hero

object more grateful can be presented to the discerning eye of reason.[25]

Barrow then concludes with an argument significantly related to Fielding's own conception of the character of the good man as fictional protagonist. In order to encourage emulation, the historian must depict the human imperfections, as well as the virtues, of his heroes; the flawless model of righteousness, of which Christ was the only instance, is not only unreal but "so perfect and high, that we may not ever reach it; looking upon it may therefore sometimes dazzle and discourage our weakness." As didactic instruments, then, patterns of imperfect goodness are preferable since we may see that "they were subject to the difficulties, which we feel; they were exposed to the perils of falling, which we fear: we may therefore hope to march on in a reasonable distance after them; we may, by help of the same grace, come near in transcribing their less exact copy."[26] Such examples visibly and effectually demonstrate that the obligations of morality are "not chimerical propositions of impossible performances; but duties . . . really practicable."[27]

A similar theory lies behind the best-loved characters of Fielding's fiction, Parson Adams and Tom Jones, and its wisdom would seem to be demonstrated when we compare these men — good, yet fallible — with such lifeless paragons as Squire Allworthy or Dr. Harrison or Richardson's Sir Charles Grandison. Perhaps with an eye to the practice of his rival Richardson, Fielding pauses in *Tom Jones* (X, 1) to criticize unnatural idealism in the portrayal of character. The reader must not, he admonishes, "condemn a character as a bad one because it is not perfectly a good one"; such paragons are false to experience: "I a little question whether mere man ever arrived at this consummate degree of excellence." In close agreement with Barrow, Fielding then declares the greater efficacy of the imperfectly virtuous hero to inspire imitation and promote morality:

Nor do I, indeed, conceive the good purposes served by inserting characters of such angelic perfection, or such diabolical depravity, in any work of invention; since, from contemplating either, the mind of man is more likely to be overwhelmed with sorrow and shame than to draw any good uses from such patterns; for in the former instance he may be both concerned and ashamed to see a pattern of excellence in his nature, which he may reasonably despair of ever arriving at. . . .

In fact, if there be enough of goodness in a character to engage the admiration and affection of a well-disposed mind, though there should appear some of those little blemishes, *quas humana parum cavit natura,* they will raise our compassion rather than our abhorrence. Indeed, nothing can be of more moral use than the imperfections which are seen in examples of this kind, since such form a kind of surprise, more apt to affect and dwell upon our minds than the faults of very vicious and wicked persons. The foibles and vices of men, in whom there is a great mixture of good, become more glaring objects from the virtues which contrast them and show their deformity. . . .[28]

Like Tom Jones, Adams has his foibles—he is quite vain of his sermons and of his ability as a schoolmaster, and he is too precariously ignorant of the ways of this world—but for all that, the good parson, at once humorous and heroic, strides triumphant along his pilgrim's road. Perhaps despite ourselves, and if only for a time, his example draws us after him.

The Good Man as Hero

It would be unwise, of course, to insist that Barrow's sermon necessarily provides the ethical rationale behind the heroes and action of *Joseph Andrews*. His position is clearly not original: the superiority of examples over precepts and of Scriptural heroes over pagan, the choice of Abraham and Joseph as representatives of true faith and temperance, the greater moral efficacy of imperfect patterns of virtue—these points are all commonplaces of the period. Nevertheless, the similarities between the content of Barrow's discourse and Fielding's practice in *Joseph Andrews* are too many and too striking to be wholly accidental.

Barrow's preference for histories recording "the lives and examples of holy men" as opposed to pagan heroes may be related, furthermore, to contemporary theories of the Christian (and specifically biblical) epic—the arguments, both in France and in England, concerning the proper subjects for heroic poetry. French critics such as Godeau, Saint-Amant, and Desmarets were especially outspoken advocates of the biblical epic, whose foundation, according to R. A. Sayce, "was the belief that the Bible offered literary themes and characters which far surpassed those of the ancient poets."[29] On the Continent, significantly for our purposes, the stories of Joseph and Abraham provided a rich mine of material for the epic.[30] In England discussion really began with the publication of Cowley's *Poems* (1656). In the important Preface, Cowley defended his unfinished biblical epic, the *Davideis*, and recommended the Scriptures as a repository of "bright and magnificent subjects." Like Barrow, he preferred the heroes of the Bible—Noah, Moses, Samson, David and Jonathan—to those of paganism. "All the *Books* of the

A Study of *Joseph Andrews*

Bible," he wrote, "are either already most admirable and exalted pieces of Poesie, or are the best *Materials* in the world for it."[31] Similarly, Milton, whom Fielding ranked with Homer and Virgil as the best of the epic poets,[32] later declared the superiority of his subject to those of the *Iliad*, *Odyssey*, and *Aeneid*. The Fall of Man, he wrote in the Preamble to *Paradise Lost*, Book IX, was an argument

> Not less but more Heroic than the wrath
> Of stern *Achilles* on his Foe pursu'd
> Thrice Fugitive about *Troy* Wall; or rage
> Of *Turnus* for *Lavinia* disespous'd,
> Or *Neptune's* ire or *Juno's* . . . (ll. 14-18)

Perhaps, as Basil Willey suggests, interest in the biblical epic was one manifestation of the search for truth in the age of Bacon and the Royal Society; in Scripture, after all, God had condescended to be a poet.[33] It is certain, however, that the examples of Cowley and Milton engendered a spate of undistinguished imitations, such performances as Samuel Wesley the elder's *The Life of Our Blessed Lord and Saviour Jesus Christ* (1693), Thomas Ellwood's *Davideis* (1712), John Henley's *Esther* (1714), the anonymous *Prae-existence* (1714), Thomas Newcomb's *The Last Judgment of Men and Angels* (1723), and Aaron Hill's *Gideon* (1749—the manuscript was completed in 1724). As more notable attempts to treat Scriptural themes in a heroic manner, we may mention as well such very different works as Milton's *Paradise Regained* (1671) and *Samson Agonistes* (1671), Dryden's *Absalom and Achitophel* (1681), and Prior's *Solomon on the Vanity of the World* (1718). Following Cowley and Milton, the critics and other commentators—Samuel Woodford, John

The Good Man as Hero

Dryden, Sir Richard Blackmore, John Dennis, and Isaac Watts, for example—also advocated the use of Christian, if not always biblical, subject matter in the epic.[34] Though opposed by the followers of Boileau, as H. T. Swedenberg observes, "the proponents of Christian materials were in the majority."[35]

If we keep in mind Fielding's mock-heroic adaptation of the Joseph-Abraham themes—and indeed we must never forget that however earnest Fielding is, he is persistently working in the *comic* mode—the tradition of the Christian epic provides further background for an understanding of *Joseph Andrews*. It is one phase of neoclassic epic theory previously unexplored by students of Fielding's "comic Epic Poem in Prose."

But let us return to our analysis of the good man. A final feature of the concept involved the application of the old analogy, both Scriptural and classical, comparing the life of a good man amid a world of vanity and vexation to that of the pilgrim exiled and wayfaring through strange and hostile lands to his true home. The theme, as Tillyard points out, was especially popular with the Puritan preachers of the seventeenth century,[36] and it is the basis of Bunyan's *Pilgrim's Progress*. The latitudinarian divines, however, also made frequent use of the traditional allegory. In his sermon "Of Contentment," Isaac Barrow thus likened the hard life of man to the rough journey of a traveler in search of a better country:

This world is a place of banishment from our first country, and the original felicity we were designed to; this life is a state of travel toward another better country, and seat of rest . . . it should not be strange to us, if in this our peregrination we do meet with rough passages, foul ways, hard lodging, scant or coarse fare.[37]

A paragraph in Bishop Hoadly's "No Continuing City Here, &c." renders the metaphor more fully, comparing life to a passage on foot and the world to the road over which we travel, finding little ease or entertainment and no fixed lodgings:

The Life of Man, in this World, is often represented, by the *Author* of this *Epistle* [i.e., St. Paul], and other sacred Writers, as the *Life* of a *Traveller*, a *Stranger*, or *Sojourner* here below: and this World itself, as the *Road* to another. And, in Truth, this is a very proper Representation of the Case. *Heaven*, that Seat of established Happiness above, is our *Home*; and ought to be so accounted by Us. Thither all our Steps ought to be tending: and through this World must we go, as through a Road, before we come to it. In our Journey, We have all the Unhappinesses of *Travellers*. We meet with an inconvenient Lodging, and ordinary Entertainment, for some Time. And if it be otherwise, yet we must certainly leave it; and no more think of settling ourselves in it, than a *Traveller* does of fixing his *Habitation* upon the most beautiful Spot of Earth he meets with in his Way; or in the best accommodated House upon his Road. The little *Rest* we have, if we have any, is, as in a *strange* Place, disturbed and interrupted with much Noise, and Hurry, and Disorder; and, like that of *Travellers*, to be left, perhaps, with the next Morning's Light; and ourselves to be called Home to a more fixt and durable State.[38]

Again, the wanderings of Abraham in Egypt and Canaan were used to exemplify this pilgrimage of the righteous man through the world. In "The Character of a Good Man" Samuel Clarke thus offers Abraham as his chief *exemplum* and compares his wanderings to the transient and uncertain life of the good man here on earth: "*He himself* did but sojourn *in the land of Promise, as in a strange country,* and *confessed that he was a Stranger and Pilgrim on the Earth.*"[39] Finally, Tillotson's sermon "Good Men Strangers and Sojourners upon Earth" cites the journeys of Abraham and other patriarchs as symbolic of the condition of the good man passing through this world, where "all is vanity and vexation of spirit," seeking "a better country."[40]

As Fielding undertook his first comic epic or "history," then, he found at hand a workable theory of the good man, potentially a convenient ethical foil to the vanity and hypocrisy he wished to expose. In Fielding's hands, of course, this material was tailored, hilariously, to suit the needs of satire; the good man, as it were, was clothed in antic dress. But Fielding's motives were earnest none the less. In their wayfaring from the corruption of the Great City toward happiness in a better country, his own Christian heroes, a virtuous footman and a benevolent parson, serve as a constant commentary upon the pretentious and uncharitable. As presented in the homilies and especially in Isaac Barrow's "Of Being Imitators of Christ," the concept of the good man as moral exemplar shares with *Pamela* and *Don Quixote* the distinction of inspiring the creation of Joseph Andrews and Abraham Adams. With regard to the meaning and structure of the novel, its importance is unrivaled.

IV

Vanity, Fortune, and the Classical Ideal

ONE OF THE strangest yet most characteristic features of modern criticism of *Joseph Andrews* is its treatment of the Wilson episode. Here, perhaps even more than with the novel as a whole, the passage of time has prevented our full appreciation of what Fielding was about. With few exceptions, the critics, depending on their sympathies, either apologize in embarrassment for the "digression"—if Fielding lacked our sophisticated notions of form, he was, after all, new at his craft—or, unabashed, accuse him outright of ineptitude. Even those who have suspected that he knew what he was doing, that the episode really does have a function within the total organization of the novel, have not been entirely helpful in identifying that function. The story of Mr. Wilson lies very near the heart of *Joseph Andrews*, both structurally and thematically. It has to do with matters of morality and the good life, with literary and ethical traditions, that once were familiar but need now to be redefined. The present chapter attempts to furnish this background; the episode itself will be taken up at length in a later section.

For the most part the conceptions that underlie the episode, two chapters that summarize the satiric and moral

Vanity, Fortune, and the Classical Ideal

content of the novel, are an amalgam of Christian and classical commonplaces; namely, *vanitas vanitatum,* the country versus the city, and Providence and free will versus Fortune — themes to be found in Ecclesiastes, Lucretius, Juvenal, Virgil, Horace, Ovid, Martial, Seneca, Cicero, Boethius, and countless sermons and poems more or less contemporary with Fielding. True wisdom or (as Fielding liked to call it) Prudence enabled one correctly to estimate these relative values.

In her exhaustive study of the sources of Gray's *Elegy,* Amy Reed has noticed in detail the abundance of seventeenth- and eighteenth-century verse on the subject of retirement from the vanity of the world. Throughout the first quarter of the latter century, she remarks, there is "the same complaint of the vanity of life, the same professed admiration for solitary retirement," subject to "the same literary influences, Lucretius, Virgil, Horace, Seneca, Martial, *Ecclesiastes, Job,* the *Psalms,* reinforced by the influence of Milton."[1] The *vanitas vanitatum* theme — *"that great Assertion, laid down in the beginning of the* ECCLESIASTES, ALL IS VANITY"[2] — was perhaps most elaborately treated in Matthew Prior's biblical poem, *Solomon on the Vanity of the World,* and most effectively in Dr. Johnson's imitation of Juvenal, *The Vanity of Human Wishes.* And of course it was a recurrent topic in the sermons, where this world was typically styled "only *deceptio visus;* a show without a substance; it doth but delude the careless spectators with false appearance; it hath nothing under it solid or stable; being laid in the balance . . . it will prove lighter than vanity itself."[3] The wisdom of disentangling oneself as much as possible from the vain and vicious affairs of this life, moreover, was the particular concern of an extensive literature, classical in inspiration, that opposed the simplicity and naturalness of rural retirement to the luxury and corruption of the city. Modified by the Christian concepts of charity and of contempt for the vanities of the world, this classical ideal of the wise and happy life informs the Wilson episode.

Behind the basic thematic antithesis of city versus country lie two distinct, yet closely related, literary traditions. The *locus classicus* of anti-urban literature is, of course, Juvenal's *Third Satire,* in which the poet's friend Umbricius, on the point of forsaking Rome for a quiet country life, relates with some bitterness a long catalogue of city vice and folly. Although the classical ideal is Juvenal's clearly implied alternative to urban existence, its more explicit delineation may be found toward the close of Virgil's *Second Georgic* (11. 458-540), beginning with a paean of praise for the life of the happy husbandmen: "O fortunatos nimium, sua si bona norint,/agricolas!" Virgil's glorification of the husbandman's way of life stressed particularly his opportunities for leisurely contemplation and the contentment of voluntary separation from the turmoil, ambition, and luxury of the great world. The life lived according to nature—simple, industrious, pious, just, carefree, and happy in the mutual love of one's family— such was the manner of the Golden Age: "aureus hanc vitam in terris Saturnus agebat" (1. 538). The theme of country versus city, or merely the exaltation of the life of retirement without its opposite, was variously sounded by Ovid, Horace, Martial, Lucretius, Seneca, Cicero, and Cato, to name but a few.

It was inevitable, of course, that the poets of England's

Vanity, Fortune, and the Classical Ideal

Augustan Age should recognize the pertinence of these values for their own times. Among the many translations and imitations of Juvenal's *Third Satire*, those by Dryden, Oldham, and Johnson are most remarkable, the last two cleverly adapting the point of the original to apply to a new Babylon—London. The related theme of retirement was equally a commonplace, occurring, for instance, in the poetry of Cowley, Prior, Parnell, Pope, Dyer, Thomson, Green, Joseph Warton, and Goldsmith, and in Shaftesbury's *The Moralists*; and its frequent appearance in the fugitive verse submitted to *The Gentleman's Magazine* further testifies to its general popularity.[4] The classical ideal in its simplest form underlies, as well, the favorite eighteenth-century genre of the pastoral, the purpose of which, according to Rapin and his followers, was "to hold up a picture of the Golden Age to a less fortunate generation."[5]

Although it had no precise parallel in Scripture, this concept of the happy life was also taken up by the homilists in stressing the vanity of earthly affairs—invariably, of course, with a Christian insistence upon the final inadequacy of even the wisest mode of life in "this kingdom of change and contingency."[6] Robert South several times located the truest earthly contentment "under the meanest cottage" with "the honest plowman";[7] for here, pre-eminently, was the happiness of a "middle condition," avoiding the pitfalls attendant upon the extremes of riches and poverty: "The honest country gentleman . . . or country farmer, have all the real benefits of nature, and the blessings of plenty, that the highest and richest grandees can pretend to. . . . And he who is not contented with such a condition must seek his happiness (if ever he have any) in another world, for Providence itself can provide no better for him in this."[8]

We may detect in the writings of the divines, however, an important qualification of this ideal. Because they emphasized the Christian's obligations to charity, the latitudinarians were reluctant to recommend the ideal of retirement without modifying it to include, paradoxically, an active involvement in the affairs of society. In contrasting the characters of John the Baptist and Christ, Bishop Hoadly asks, "Who would not be glad to retire from a World of Noise and Impertinence, of Ignorance and Folly, and, what is worst of all, of Wickedness and Impiety?" But he insists also upon the individual's duty to contribute to the well-being of his neighbor; retirement is permissible only if it does not prevent the fulfillment of "any of the Duties strictly owing to Human *Society*."[9] As attested by the example of Mr. Wilson, whose charitable offices to his neighbors Fielding carefully notices, Hoadly's Christian compromise with the classical ideal is practical, in fact even preferable. It perfectly explains the antithetical attitudes we are meant to hold toward the different solutions of the benevolent Mr. Wilson and the misanthropic Man of the Hill in *Tom Jones*.

Another recurring theme of Christian ethics and theology accounts for the specific pattern of Wilson's rake's progress through London society. Wilson's flirtation with the club of political philosophers, who chose to see "the Falsehood of that very antient but simple Tenet, that there is such a Being as a Deity in the Universe" (III, 3), is more than a passing incident in the long catalogue of London vanities. It is indicative of the moral blindness that leads him ignorantly through the trials of prosperity

Vanity, Fortune, and the Classical Ideal

and adversity to eventual despair and causes him erroneously to place his trust in Fortune rather than in Providence.

The main source for the Christian defense of Providence and free will as opposed to Fortune is, of course, Boethius' *Consolation of Philosophy*, a book that Parson Adams likes to quote and recommend (III, 11). Indeed, before his spiritual rescue by the Lady Philosophy, Boethius' troubled state of mind while awaiting death in prison bears a broad resemblance to Wilson's condition, hopelessly languishing in debtor's prison until the charity of his future wife gains his liberty: each must learn the folly of trusting in Fortune and the true wisdom of recognizing God's Providence, which tests and corrects the individual soul through prosperity and adversity. An unfailing awareness of this truth also sustained Job and the author of Ecclesiastes (VII:14). There is no need to document at length the basic Christian tenet that God's Providence extends to the most trifling circumstances, even to "a thing, of all others, the most casual and fortuitous, such as is the casting of lots."[10] In a passage to which Fielding alluded in *Amelia* (I, 3), Samuel Clarke condemned as *"Atheistical"* those who "directly *deny* either the *Being* or the *Providence* of God."[11]

The thinking of the divines regarding the special functions of the providential trials of prosperity and adversity may not be so familiar. According to Isaac Barrow, an abundance of the goods of fortune is dangerous in the extreme:

They puff up our minds with vain and false conceits. . . . They render us insensible and forgetful of God, of ourselves, of piety and virtue, of all that is good and worthy of us. . . . They

A Study of *Joseph Andrews*

immerse our souls in all the follies of pride, in all the filths of luxury, in all the mischiefs emergent from sloth and stupidity; they are *The root of all evils* unto us, and the greatest obstructions of our true happiness, rendering salvation almost impossible, and heaven in a manner inaccessible to us.[12]

After a long and spiritually enervating course of prosperity, the function of adversity—God's "severe medicine"—is to cure the sick soul, to restore its good health by promoting humility and repentance and a judicious contempt of earthly vanities. Samuel Clarke writes as follows:

Such is the deceitfulness of mens Hearts, that in a long course of uninterrupted Prosperity, this secret Pride is apt to grow insensibly, even upon those who do not affect to practise Iniquity. The almost only certain and effectual remedy of which Evil, and the proper Preservative against it, is that mixture of *Afflictions* and Disappointments in the World, which, by the wise order and appointment of Providence, puts men in mind of their own Weakness and Infirmity, brings them to a right Sense of themselves and of their dependence upon God, puts them upon serious consideration of the true State and Circumstances of things, and is therefore in Scripture called the *Discipline* and *Instruction* of the Lord.[13]

In a passage that perfectly summarizes the concept, Barrow similarly describes affliction as the school of wisdom and the purge of vanity:

Adversity . . . in true judgment, nothing commonly is more necessary, more wholesome, more useful and beneficial to us; nothing is more needful, or conducible to the health of our soul, and to our real happiness, than it: it is the school of wisdom, wherein our minds are disciplined and improved in the knowledge of the best things, whence it is termed παιδεία, that is,

Vanity, Fortune, and the Classical Ideal

instructive chastisement. . . . It is the academy wherein virtue is acquired and exercised. . . .

It is the furnace of the soul, wherein it is tried, cleansed, and refined from the dross of vain conceits, of perverse humours, of vicious distempers. . . .

It is the method whereby God reclaimeth sturdy sinners to goodness. . . .[14]

Without the test of adversity, Barrow continues, no man can become truly wise or good; he will be ignorant of himself and unable to discipline his passions. True wisdom will be denied him who is glutted with the goods of this world:

What but deprivation of these things can lay open the vanity, the deceitfulness, and slipperiness of them? What but crosses and disappointments here can withdraw our minds from a fond admiration, and eager affection toward this world?[15]

Without a proper understanding, however, that the trials of adversity are occasioned, not by blind Chance or Fortune, but by the benevolent and corrective Providence of God, affliction will end in despair, not wisdom.[16]

After a long and painful, yet instructive, involvement in the vanities of the Great City, Mr. Wilson earns his reward. The ideal of wisdom and happiness that his story represents is the natural expression of these familiar classical and Christian concepts.

Fielding's Ethics

To grasp the moral implications of satire, we must hold in mind two distinct thematic layers that function concomitantly: a thesis attacking vice and folly, and an antithesis comprising a positive ethical alternative, the standard against which the satirized are measured.

The satiric thesis of *Joseph Andrews,* called to our attention in the author's Preface, may be defined as "the true Ridiculous" in society—affectation and its twin causes, vanity and hypocrisy. In practice, however, the object of Fielding's savage indignation was simply selfishness in its various manifestations, a quality that was for him usually synonymous with vanity, understood in a darker sense than its use in the Preface would imply. "Vanity," remarks Mr. Wilson, "is the worst of Passions, and more apt to contaminate the Mind than any other: for, as Selfishness is much more general than we please to allow it, so it is natural to hate and envy those who stand between us and the Good we desire" (III, 3). And in *The Champion* (April 15, 1740), Fielding had declared that "vanity is the true source of ridicule"; "No passion hath so much the ascendant in the composition of human nature as vanity," which, in its worst form, is "at the bottom of most villainy, and the cause of most human miseries."[1] But perhaps the significance of the term to Fielding's satiric rationale is

Fielding's Ethics

best revealed in a burlesque apostrophe in *Joseph Andrews*; here vanity connotes much more than merely "affecting false Characters" or "Ostentation," the meaning to which Fielding apparently confines it in his Preface:

> O Vanity! How little is thy Force acknowledged, or thy Operations discerned! How wantonly dost thou deceive Mankind under different Disguises! Sometimes thou dost wear the Face of Pity, sometimes of Generosity: nay, thou hast the Assurance even to put on those glorious Ornaments which belong only to heroick Virtue. Thou odious, deformed Monster! whom Priests have railed at, Philosophers despised, and Poets ridiculed. Is there a Wretch so abandoned as to own thee for an Acquaintance in publick?—yet, how few will refuse to enjoy thee in private? nay, thou are the Pursuit of most Men through their Lives. The greatest Villanies are daily practised to please thee; nor is the meanest Thief below, or the greatest Heroe above, thy notice. Thy Embraces are often the sole Aim and sole Reward of the private Robbery and the plundered Province. It is to pamper up thee, thou Harlot, that we attempt to withdraw from others what we do not want, or to withhold from them what they do. All our Passions are thy Slaves. Avarice itself is often no more than thy Handmaid, and even Lust thy Pimp. The Bully Fear, like a Coward, flies before thee, and Joy and Grief hide their Heads in thy Presence. (I, 15)

In this sense, vanity is to Fielding what self-love is to Barrow and the latitudinarian opposition to Hobbes and Mandeville—the chief vice subsuming all others, the root of uncharitableness. It is the ultimate object of his corrective ridicule, though his particular target may be the lust of Lady Booby or Mrs. Slipslop, or the avarice of Parson Trulliber or Peter Pounce or Mrs. Tow-wouse.

A Study of *Joseph Andrews*

The key to the satire of *Joseph Andrews,* however, lies in the ethos of the novel, a standard held up as a foil setting off the moral degeneracy of the age and embodied especially in the innocent quixotism of Abraham Adams. It is scarcely by accident that Fielding's good parson, like his namesake an exemplar of true faith and charity, performs in this Christian epic of the road a function closely analogous to that of the *persona* of formal satire. That is, he operates both separately and simultaneously in the three characters that Maynard Mack attributes to the satirist: (1) the *vir bonus* or moral man; (2) the *naïf,* simple and unsophisticated, passing implicit judgment upon the immorality that bewilders him; and (3) the *hero,* indignant and courageous, defending virtue and the public good.[2] At the moment, however, we are less concerned with Adams' role as a satiric vehicle than with Fielding's conception of him as the Christian hero, the representative *par excellence* of the two virtues that his author, following the latitudinarians, placed at the heart of morality—good nature and charity.

Formulated as early as *The Champion,* Fielding's version of the familiar benevolist concept of good nature remains the substance of his definition of the moral man. It is the energizing principle behind the characters of Heartfree, Tom Jones, Squire Allworthy, Captain Booth, Doctor Harrison, and, pre-eminently, Parson Adams. It is misleading, however, to describe this principle, as W. R. Irwin has done, as "nothing more than a simplified, informal, common-sense version of the elaborate doctrine of benevolism."[3] Fielding is in general accord with the latitudinarian position outlined earlier: he insists that true charity, essential to salvation, is the fruit of a sympathetic

Fielding's Ethics

compassion natural to man. Yet his conception must also be distinguished from the promiscuous sentimentalism into which the benevolist ethic degenerated. Fielding, for one, would not have missed Sterne's irony in the incident of Uncle Toby and the trapped fly or Yorick and the caged starling, with which it is instructive to compare Tom Jones' imperiling life and limb to restore Sophia's songbird to captivity. Because it was primarily a social virtue, Fielding's good nature, like that of Addison,[4] was also rational, complementing pity with good judgment as to its objects.

Like the latitudinarians in his reaction to Hobbes and Calvinism, Fielding took a predominantly optimistic view of human nature. Throughout his career as journalist and novelist, he vigorously attacked "these political philosophers"—that is, the school of Hobbes, Rochefoucauld, and Mandeville—who represented man as a creature "depraved, and totally bad."[5] His usual way of dismissing "those authors, who have set human nature in a very vile and detestable light" was to turn their arguments back upon them: "Those who deduce actions, apparently good, from evil causes, can trace them only through the windings of their own hearts; and while they attempt to draw an ugly picture of human nature, they must of necessity copy the deformity from their own minds."[6] In *Tom Jones* (VI, 1) he condemned "that modern doctrine" which alarmed the world by declaring "that there were no such things as virtue or goodness really existing in human nature, and . . . deduced our best actions from pride." Such speculations only arise from searching into "the nastiest of all places, A BAD MIND. . . . The truth-finder, having raked out that jakes, his own mind, and being there capable of tracing no ray of divinity, nor anything virtuous or good, or lovely, or loving, very fairly, honestly, and logically concludes that no such things exist in the whole creation."[7] Particularly irritating was the cynical egoism of "that charming fellow Mandevil . . . who hath represented human nature in a picture of the highest deformity." Fielding, who later took exception specifically to the doctrine of Mandeville's *Essay on Charity*,[8] has Captain Booth explain his objections:

"He hath left out of his system the best passion which the mind can possess, and attempts to derive the effects or energies of that passion from the base impulses of pride or fear. Whereas it is as certain that love exists in the mind of man as that its opposite hatred doth; and the same reasons will equally prove the existence of the one as the existence of the other."[9]

But it is Tom Jones (VIII, 15) whose arguments against the misanthropy of the Man of the Hill best express his author's criticism of both Hobbes and the Calvinists:

"If there was, indeed, much more wickedness in the world than there is, it would not prove such general assertions against human nature, since much of this arrives by mere accident, and many a man who commits evil is not totally bad and corrupt in his heart. In truth, none seem to have any title to assert human nature to be necessarily and universally evil, but those whose own minds afford them one instance of this natural depravity. . . ."[10]

To determine Fielding's true estimate of human nature from the many contradictory assertions that appear in his writings is not an easy task. In a recent essay, for example, George Sherburn has adduced evidence on both sides of

Fielding's Ethics

the old questions of environment or heredity, free will or determinism.[11] Despite Fielding's somewhat confusing subscription to the popular contemporary theory of a predominant passion, a fact that has led at least one scholar to posit an indebtedness to Hume,[12] his over-all agreement with the latitudinarians seems clear. Although declaring the naturalness of the social affections, the liberal divines did not argue for the absolute innate goodness of men. Isaac Barrow, we recall, recognized varying degrees of good nature among men, and, as Christians, these writers admitted man's weakness since the Fall. Thus, in his attack on Hobbes and the Calvinists in *The Champion* (December 11, 1739), Fielding assured his readers that, "though I am unwilling to look on human nature as a mere sink of iniquity, I am far from insinuating that it is a state of perfection."[13] He was not blind to the reality of malice, which proceeds from "the malignity of our natures" and is motivated by a principle directly contrary to good nature—"a delight in mischief."[14] Late in his career as a magistrate, while contemplating the seemingly gratuitous cruelty of Elizabeth Canning's abductors, Fielding sadly asked:

How many cruelties, indeed, do we daily hear of, to which it seems not easy to assign any other motive than barbarity itself? In serious and sorrowful truth, doth not history, as well as our own experience, afford us too great reasons to suspect, that there is in some minds a sensation directly opposite to that of benevolence, and which delights and feeds itself with acts of cruelty and inhumanity?[15]

Like a good Christian, he attributed these seeds of ill nature to Original Sin: to Adam's eating the forbidden fruit, he said, "we owe all the evil and miseries to which our nature is now subject."[16]

To explain the apparent variety in the characters of men, the familiar psychological theory of the passions was convenient. In the short poem "To John Hayes, Esq.," Fielding described human nature as a composition of conflicting humors; he observed

> How passions blended on each other fix,
> How vice with virtues, faults with graces mix;
> How passions opposite, as sour to sweet,
> Shall in one bosom at one moment meet,
> With various luck for victory contend,
> And now shall carry, and now lose their end.[17]

Like Pope, however, he usually extended this concept to interpret the actions of men as stemming from the impulses of a single predominant passion, a doctrine logically conducive to determinism. The narrator of the allegorical *Journey from this World to the Next* (I, 6), accordingly, depicts the prenatal preparation of the spirits in Elysium: each is made to drink from two phials — the "Pathetic Potion," containing the various humors, and the "Nousphoric Decoction," source of the rational faculties. The Potion is represented as "a mixture of all the passions, but in no exact proportion, so that sometimes one predominates and sometimes another; nay, often in the hurry of making up, one particular ingredient is, as we were informed, left out."[18] Only through the acknowledgment of "some unacquired, original distinction, in the nature or soul of one man, from that of another," Fielding felt, may we account for the markedly different inclinations to good or evil

Fielding's Ethics

among children, let us say, of the same background and education.[19] This idea is dramatically illustrated in the novels by the contrasting characters of Tom Jones and Blifil, and Amelia and her sister Betty. That Fielding, however, was also aware of the adaptability of this theory to the dangerous doctrine of fatalism, which he emphatically rejected, is clear from his representation of Captain Booth's spiritual impasse: " 'My chief doubt was founded on this —that as men appeared to me to act entirely from their passions, their actions could have neither merit nor demerit.' "[20] The lesson that Booth at last learned, of course, had been recommended much earlier in *The Champion* (February 2, 1739/40)—"that glorious precept *vince teipsum*," or the ability of the individual, by reason and will, to direct and order the passions.[21]

Although Fielding did not, in any absolute sense, admit the innate goodness of men, he did maintain that, of the "passions blended" in human nature, love and benevolence and compassion were very real components, operative in some men more strongly than in others, but present in all to some degree. As a reformer, he strove to further this natural propensity to virtue by attacking the deterrents to the good life—bad education, bad custom, bad example —and by recommending the voluntary cultivation of the generous affections.

"The nature of man is far from being in itself evil [remarks Dr. Harrison in close paraphrase of Isaac Barrow]; it abounds with benevolence, charity, and pity, coveting praise and honor, and shunning shame and disgrace. Bad education, bad habits, and bad customs, debauch our nature, and drive it headlong as it were into vice. The governors of the world, and I am afraid the priesthood, are answerable for the badness of it.

Instead of discouraging wickedness to the utmost of their power, both are too apt to connive at it."[22]

True good nature, pure and simple, results only when the benevolent passions predominate. In *An Inquiry into the Causes of the Late Increase of Robbers,* Fielding remarks: "Indeed the passion of love or benevolence, whence this admirable disposition arises, seems to be the only human passion that is in itself simply and absolutely good";[23] and in *The Covent-Garden Journal,* No. 29 (April 11, 1752), he hails it as "that excellent Temper of Mind, that Passion which is the Perfection of human Nature, of which the Delight is in doing Good."[24] But the seeds of this innate goodness, as Dr. Harrison indicated, are latent in everyone. It is a social affection, involving the individual sympathetically and selflessly in the affairs of humanity and so natural to man that those who deny its impulses "live in a constant opposition to their own nature, and are no less monsters than the most wanton abortions, or extravagant births."[25] This it is that constitutes "the most essential barrier between us and our neighbors the brutes."[26]

Because of human frailty and a corrupt environment, however, true good nature is "rarely found."[27] Fielding, nonetheless, frequently insisted with the latitudinarians that man, assisted by a wholesome education and duly inspired by the "rod and sweetmeat" incentives of religion, could *voluntarily* achieve a high degree of moral excellence. It is this conviction that underlies the Pelagian content of his writing. Even in one of his darkest moments, recalling during his final illness the humiliation he suffered while being carried aboard the ship that transported him to Lisbon, he could declare that human nature need only be "polish'd and refin'd . . . to produce that perfection of which it is susceptible."²⁸ Both early and late he held the life of benevolence, necessary to salvation, to be accessible to all—if not from the instinctive compulsions of purest good nature, at least from choice. God, he said in *The Champion* (March 27, 1740), is

> . . . the best-natured being in the universe; the more therefore we cultivate the sweet disposition in our minds, the nearer we draw to divine perfection; to which we should be the more strongly incited, as it is that which we may approach the nearest to. All his other attributes throw us immediately out of sight, but this virtue lies in will, and not at all in power.²⁹

Although he credited the theory of the passions in explanation of the variety of human actions, he thus carefully avoided the fallacy of fatalism that nearly ensnared Captain Booth. Writing near the end of his career, in *The Covent-Garden Journal*, No. 16 (February 25, 1752), he reasserted the moral responsibility of the individual: "In the worthiest human Minds, there are some small innate Seeds of Malignity, which it is greatly in our Power either to suffocate and suppress, or to forward and improve their Growth, 'till they blossom and bear their poisonous Fruit"; and addressing his reader with regard to the extremes of good and ill nature, he added "that it is greatly within his Power to resemble which of the two he pleases, in other Words to imitate the most benevolent and virtuous, or the most wicked and base of all Beings."³⁰ Against the "morose and austere" doctrine of a rigorous Calvinism—perhaps with Whitefield in mind—he endorsed the optimistic theology of the liberal divines: "I say, with Dr. Barrow, *Let us improve and advance our Nature to the utmost Perfection of which it is capable,* I mean by doing all the Good we can; and surely that Nature which seems to partake of the divine Goodness in this World, is the most likely to partake of the divine Happiness in the next."[31] An awareness of this Pelagian aspect of Fielding's thought is important, for it defines his views with regard to the problems of free will and determinism, and provides the rationale behind his tireless efforts, as both magistrate and novelist, toward social reform.

Even though Fielding's concept of good nature comprehended the idea of an innate moral sense that Shaftesbury had popularized, the essential Christianity of his position is apparent from his heavy emphasis upon the need for corrective education and the additional persuasives of future rewards and punishments. Writing in *Amelia* (IX, 9) about the benevolent proprietor of the Vauxhall Gardens, he confirmed "the truth of an observation which I have read in some ethic writer, that a truly elegant taste is generally accompanied with an excellency of heart; or, in other words, that true virtue is, indeed, nothing else but true taste."[32] But the moral weakness of the generality of mankind required discipline. What Fielding called "a wholesome severity" in the rearing of children was needed to purge, or at least to suppress, vicious inclinations.[33] Education, he remarked in *The Jacobite's Journal,* No. 22 (April 30, 1748), "may serve for all good Purposes, and . . . may so cultivate the Human Mind, that every Seed of Good in Human Nature may be reared up to full Perfection and Maturity; while all which is of evil Tendency is weeded, and, as it were, pluck'd by the Roots from the youthful Disposition, before it spreads, and is strengthened by Time." The benefit of a proper instruction and discipline of the young, so vividly demonstrated by the upbringing of Amelia's children,[34] was the nourishment of the good-natured affections and the repression of vice. Echoing a statement of Quintilian quoted earlier in *The Champion* (November 20, 1739), Fielding summarized his position with regard to the relative functions of nature and art in the formation of character: "Tho' Nature however must give the Seeds, Art may cultivate them. To improve or to depress their Growth is greatly within the Power of Education."[35] So firmly did Fielding believe in this "Power" that in two important numbers of *The Covent-Garden Journal*, Nos. 42 and 56, he traced the prevalence of vanity and folly in English society to faulty standards of education. The wholesome discipline of the classics and "Good Breeding" was being replaced by the fashionable debauchery of the town and the Grand Tour. Indeed, in the latter essay, important for its bearing on his theory of satire, Fielding located the source of "the Ridiculous" in "that Method so general in this Kingdom of giving no Education to the Youth of both Sexes."[36]

Of equal importance in supplementing natural compulsions to virtue were the "rod and sweetmeat" incentives of religion. Here, especially, Fielding's realistic estimate of the limitations of good nature as a universal moral imperative differs from Shaftesbury's speculative idealism. One of several reasons for Fielding's disapproval of *Pamela* was its mercenary moral of "virtue rewarded" *in this life*— a comfortable doctrine, he remarks in *Tom Jones* (XV, 1), "to which we have but one objection, namely, that it is not true."[37] The virtuous man, he had declared some months before the publication of Richardson's novel, might even rejoice, philosophically, over temporal injustice, for

A Study of *Joseph Andrews*

"it furnishes him with a noble argument for the certainty of a future state. . . . It is inconsistent with the justice of a supremely wise and good being, to suffer his honest and worthy endeavours to go unrewarded."[38] Religion, moreover, was of practical social importance as the final check to immorality. In reply to Booth's statement of psychological determinism, Dr. Harrison, though evading the real issue, argues for the superior wisdom of Christianity over mere philosophy:

"If men act, as I believe they do, from their passions, it would be fair to conclude that religion to be true which applies immediately to the strongest of these passions, hope and fear; choosing rather to rely on its rewards and punishments than on that native beauty of virtue which some of the ancient philosophers thought proper to recommend to their disciples."[39]

Similarly, in drawing up plans for a county workhouse, Fielding, in agreement with the arguments of Archbishop Tillotson's "The Advantage of Religion to Society," made devotional observances a part of the daily regimen. Without the compelling incentives to moral behavior that Christianity provides, the majority of men, he felt, would choose "to gratify the evil inclinations" of their passions:

. . . but heaven and hell when well rung in the ears of those who have not yet learnt that there are no such places, and who will give some attention to what they hear, are by no means words of little or no signification. Hope and fear, two very strong and active passions, will hardly find a fuller or more adequate object to amuse and employ them.[40]

To attain the high pitch of morality of which they were capable, most men required stronger inducements than

Fielding's Ethics

those supplied by nature. There were limits to how far Fielding would carry his belief in the innate goodness of man. Not everyone deserved the epithet "good-natured" —as Peter Pounce, Jonathan Wild, Blifil, Amelia's sister, and a host of other characters from the novels clearly attest. It is a word that he used carefully and advisedly. Let us, then, take a closer look at this virtue that distinguishes Fielding's heroes—Parson Adams above all—and that he represents as the indispensable requisite of the completely moral man.

In the introductory chapter to Book XIII of *Tom Jones*, Fielding revealed the ethical orientation of his novels by invoking the four Muses of the prose epic—Genius, Learning, Experience, and Humanity. The last he addresses as follows:

> And thou, almost the constant attendant on true genius, Humanity, bring all thy tender sensations. . . . Not without these the tender scene is painted. From these alone proceed the noble disinterested friendship, the melting love, the generous sentiment, the ardent gratitude, the soft compassion, the candid opinion; and all those strong energies of a good mind, which fill the moistened eyes with tears, the glowing cheeks with blood, and swell the heart with tides of grief, joy, and benevolence.[41]

Fielding's customary name for the virtue here invoked was "good-nature," a term that he defined frequently and at length. In the verse essay, "Of Good-Nature," first published in its entirety in the *Miscellanies*, he asks: "What is good-nature?"

> Is it a foolish weakness in the breast,
> As some who know, or have it not, contest?

> Or is it rather not the mighty whole,
> Full composition of a virtuous soul?
> Is it not virtue's self? A flower so fine,
> It only grows in soils almost divine.

Essentially, he continues, it is "the glorious lust of doing good":

> The heart that finds its happiness to please
> Can feel another's pain, and taste his ease;
> The cheek that with another's joy can glow,
> Turn pale and sicken with another's woe;
> Free from contempt and envy, he who deems
> Justly of life's two opposite extremes,
> Who to make all and each man truly bless'd
> Doth all he can and wishes all the rest[.] [42]

Or, as he elsewhere expresses it:

Good-nature is that benevolent and amiable temper of mind, which disposes us to feel the misfortunes, and enjoy the happiness of others; and, consequently, pushes us on to promote the latter, and prevent the former; and that without any abstract contemplation on the beauty of virtue, and without the allurements or terrors of religion.[43]

From these definitions, the position of the concept in the benevolist tradition should be apparent. To begin with, Fielding's good nature must be sharply distinguished from the very different notion of benevolence to be found in the Stoic philosophers, whom at least one scholar, Maria Joesten, has proposed as the source of his ethics. However much he might admire the doctrinal philanthropy of the Stoics, Fielding, like the latitudinarians, had no patience with their philosophical contempt of the affections. The altruism of the *vir honestus* was active, but it was too cold, unfeeling, and detached—based less on charity than on the abstract considerations of philosophy. Fielding's objections to Stoicism stemmed both from his own good sense and from his religion. The Stoic's stress upon insensitive self-sufficiency in the face of misfortune might at times be desirable,[44] but, though admirable in theory, it was impractical; and his disdain of even the benevolent affections was contrary to Christian love. In *Amelia* (VIII, 10) Captain Booth's criticism of the Stoic philosopher whom he meets in the sponging house clarifies the first reservation:

"You have expressed yourself extremely well," cries Booth; "and I entirely agree with the justice of your sentiments; but, however true all this may be in theory, I still doubt its efficacy in practice. And the cause of the difference between these two is this; that we reason from our heads, but act from our hearts. . . . Nothing can differ more widely than wise men and fools in their estimation of things; but, as both act from their uppermost passion, they both often act alike."[45]

No better illustration of the truth of this observation can be found in Fielding than the failure of Parson Adams' Christian Stoicism to sustain him when he learns of the supposed drowning of his son (IV, 8). Fielding's second objection is best rendered in *The Covent-Garden Journal*, No. 29 (April 11, 1752):

We will rise therefore one Step from the odious to the insipid Character, from those who delight in doing Mischief, to those who have little or no Delight either in the Good or Harm which happeneth to others. Men of this Stamp are so taken up, in contemplating themselves, that the Virtues or Vices, the Happiness or Misery of the rest of Mankind scarce ever employ their Thoughts. This is a Character, however truly contemptible it may be, which hath not wanted its Admirers among the Antients. These Men have been called Philosophers, and in the heathen Systems they might deserve that Name; but in the sublimer Schools of the Christian Dispensation, they are so far from being entitled to any Honours, that they will be called to a severe Account (those especially who have received very considerable Talents of any Kind) for converting solely to their own Use, what was entrusted only to their Care for the general Good.[46]

With this in mind we may compare, for instance, the contrasting descriptions of Tom Jones and Colonel James in *Amelia*:

In fact, poor Jones was one of the best-natured fellows alive, and had all that weakness which is called compassion, and which distinguishes this imperfect character from that noble firmness of mind which rolls a man, as it were, within himself, and, like a polished bowl, enables him to run through the world without being once stopped by the calamities which happen to others.

About James, Fielding writes: "His mind was formed of those firm materials of which nature formerly hammered out the Stoic, and upon which the sorrows of no man living could make an impression."[47]

With the liberal divines against the Stoic contempt of the passions, Fielding thus ideally places the motivation for charity in the benevolent social affections, the naturally empathic disposition of the good-natured man. Because he suffers with the wretched and delights with the fortunate, the pain that he feels in the presence of misery urges him to take active measures to alleviate distress and pro-

Fielding's Ethics

mote happiness. Good nature, Fielding writes in *An Inquiry into the Causes of the Late Increase of Robbers,* far from being contemptible, merits the highest applause:

> It is certain that a tender-hearted and compassionate disposition, which inclines men to pity and feel the misfortunes of others, and which is, even for its own sake, incapable of involving any man in ruin and misery, is of all tempers of mind the most amiable; and though it seldom receives much honour, is worthy of the highest.[48]

It is important, too, to understand that the benevolence of the good-natured man, as Fielding declares above, is not the fruit of "any abstract contemplation on the beauty of virtue" or the merely politic fulfillment of the obligations of religion. While others are charitable from the hope of reward in the hereafter, or from intellectual semi-esthetic meditations after the manner of Shaftesbury's platonism, the man of good nature, like Squire Allworthy, acts spontaneously, impelled by "a heart that hungers after goodness."[49] Accordingly, rare though it may be, true good nature is the one and indispensable *natural* predisposition to virtue, itself defined in *The Champion* (January 3, 1739/40) as "a delight in doing good."[50]

Again, in his *An Inquiry into the Causes of the Late Increase of Robbers,* Fielding distinguished between the good-natured individual's innate compulsions to charity and the more artificially prompted benevolence of the generality of men:

> The natural energies of this temper are indeed the very virtues principally inculcated in our excellent religion; and those who, because they are natural, have denied them the name of virtues seem not, I think, to be aware of the direct and impious

tendency of a doctrine that denies all merit to a mind which is naturally, I may say necessarily, good.[51]

Good nature is thus instinctive and independent of the dictates of philosophy and religion, though it is ultimately incomplete without the latter. Discussing the characters of Thwackum and Square, Fielding reveals that their errors principally consist in a too strict preoccupation with narrow systems of morality to the neglect of their own hearts: "Had not Thwackum too much neglected virtue, and Square religion, in the composition of their several systems, and *had not both utterly discarded all natural goodness of heart,* they had never been represented as the objects of derision in this history."[52]

The characteristics of Fielding's good nature, then, closely correspond to three of the four principal features that R. S. Crane has proposed as the core of the benevolist ethic of the latitudinarians: (1) its expression is an active, universal benevolence; (2) its motivation is in the sympathetic emotions of compassion and pity; and (3) its source is the natural goodness of the heart. Fielding's version of the concept makes room as well for the fourth aspect of the sentimentalist tradition, what Crane calls the "Self-approving Joy" that is the personal recompense for the good man's labors in behalf of others. There is delight, Fielding had said, in doing good, a sentiment he rendered more fully in a letter to his friend and patron Lyttelton (August 29, 1749):

There is a great Pleasure in Gratitude tho it is second I believe to that of Benevolence: for of all the Delights upon Earth none can equal the Raptures which a good Mind feels on conferring

Fielding's Ethics

Happiness on those whom we think worthy of it. This is the sweetest ingredient in Power.[53]

Tom Jones puts the idea more effusively as he assures the lawyer Dowling of his indifference to the hollow satisfactions of material comfort:

"What is the poor pride arising from a magnificent house, a numerous equipage, a splendid table, and from all the other advantages or appearances of fortune, compared to the warm, solid content, the swelling satisfaction, the thrilling transports, and the exulting triumphs which a good mind enjoys in the contemplation of a generous, virtuous, noble, benevolent action."[54]

The tacit personal appeal in these statements is in accord with the chief utilitarian strain in the benevolist ethic, a "strain of egoistic hedonism," to use Crane's phraseology,[55] by which the latitudinarians attempted to reconcile the potent arguments of Hobbes to their own position. In *The Covent-Garden Journal*, No. 44 (June 2, 1752), for instance, Fielding in a manner identifies self-love and social:

To pursue that which is most capable of giving him Happiness, is indeed the Interest of every Man; and there are many who find great Pleasure in emptying their Purses with this View, to one who hath no other Satisfaction than in filling it. Now what can give greater Happiness to a good Mind, than the Reflexion on having relieved the Misery or contributed to the well being, of his Fellow-Creature.[56]

But it is Isaac Barrow, in a passage quoted in *The Covent-Garden Journal*, No. 29 (April 11, 1752), who best summarizes this less strictly disinterested aspect of benevolism:

A Study of *Joseph Andrews*

"A Man may be VIRTUOUSLY VOLUPTUOUS, AND A LAUDABLE EPICURE BY DOING MUCH GOOD."[57]

Because of his generous, open heart, simplicity is the characteristic of the good-natured man. He is especially exposed and susceptible to the wiles of the self-seeking and hypocritical. In *The Champion* (February 21, 1739/40) Fielding said with regret:

> Honest and undesigning men of very good understanding would be always liable to the attacks of cunning and artful knaves, into whose snares we are as often seduced by the openness and goodness of the heart, as by the weakness of the head. True wisdom is commonly attended with a simplicity of manners, which betrays a worthy man to a tricking shuffler, of a much inferior capacity.[58]

As further warning, he composed his *Essay on the Knowledge of the Characters of Men,* a full exposition of hypocrisy in its several guises, as a kind of *vade mecum* for the protection of the good-natured, "since that open disposition, which is the surest indication of an honest and upright heart, chiefly renders us liable to be imposed on by craft and deceit."[59] Instances of such imposition, a recurrent theme in Fielding's depiction of villainy, abound in the novels. Jonathan Wild's malevolent persecution of Heartfree, for example, is conducted under the mask of friendship; and Blifil's continued deception of Allworthy goes undetected through some fifteen books of *Tom Jones.* And in his insipid comedy, *The Fathers,* Fielding dramatized the gulling of the good-natured hero, Mr. Boncour, by his family and friends.

Recognizing this vulnerable side to the good man, and anxious as well that the social objectives of the benevolist

Fielding's Ethics

ethic might not be frustrated by an indiscriminate clemency, Fielding emphasized the importance of good judgment or prudence to true good nature. Because a predatory hypocrisy, he observed, is ever ready

> to betray them by means of their own goodness, it becomes the good-natured and tender-hearted man to be watchful over his own temper; to restrain the impetuosity of his benevolence, carefully to select the objects of his passion, and not by too unbounded and indiscriminate an indulgence to give the reins to a courser which will infallibly carry him into the ambuscade of the enemy.

By extending compassion promiscuously to hardened criminals, for example, good nature could become "highly prejudicial to . . . society"; and Fielding, the Bow-Street justice, continues: "To desire to save these wolves in society may arise from benevolence, but it must be the benevolence of a child or a fool, who, from want of sufficient reason, mistakes the true objects of his passion, as a child doth."[60] Even charity could become a vice if, let us say, alms were squandered foolishly upon common beggars to the increase of idleness and the detriment of the general welfare. "This Kind of Bounty," Fielding cautioned in *The Covent-Garden Journal*, No. 44 (June 2, 1752), "is a Crime against the Public."[61]

This rationalistic element distinguishes Fielding's conception of good nature from the cult of sensibility. Although he ordinarily approved "the pleasure of tenderness,"[62] he maintained the need for the benevolent man to be circumspect in choosing the objects of his compassion —a precaution necessary not only to his own welfare but also to that of society. There is a difference between the sentimental fool, which Mr. Boncour narrowly escapes being, and the truly good-natured man, a difference residing in a Lockean strain in the concept—that is, good judgment:

> This Power . . . is no other than the Distinction of Right from Wrong; or as Mr. *Lock* hath more accurately describ'd it, "The separating carefully Ideas wherein can be found the least Difference, thereby to avoid being misled by Similitude, and by Affinity to take one Thing for another."[63]

In his earliest definition of good nature in *The Champion* (March 27, 1740), Fielding stressed the importance of this rational faculty:

> Good-nature is not that weakness which, without distinction, affects both the virtuous and the base, and equally laments the punishment of villainy, with the disappointment of merit; for as this admirable quality respects the whole, so it must give up the particular, to the good of the general. . . . Good-nature requires a distinguishing faculty, which is another word for judgment, and is perhaps the sole boundary between wisdom and folly; it is impossible for a fool, who hath no distinguishing faculty, to be good-natured.[64]

The ultimate objective of Fielding's ethic was, first and last, the practical benefit of society, "the good of the general." Accordingly, a fundamental feature of his benevolism is the significant interrelationship between heart and head, sensibility and judgment. By the punishment of crimes against the commonwealth, the hangman's office, "if properly employed, may be in truth the best natured, as well as the highest post of honour in the kingdom."[65] After a careful weighing of mitigating circumstances, Tom Jones acted well in setting free the highwayman; but

Fielding's Ethics

Squire Allworthy sharply rebukes his "mistaken mercy" to Blifil as being typical of that weakness that is "very pernicious to society, as it encourages vice."[66] When confronted with villainy, Fielding firmly insisted, "the passions of the man are to give way to the principles of the magistrate."[67]

Although good nature itself is basically a natural and secular virtue, Fielding chose to place it in a specifically Christian context. While not so sovereign and selfless as the *agape* of the New Testament, which teaches forgiveness of injuries, it yet bears marks of correspondence to that Christian ideal. Compare, for example, the following description of good nature in *The Champion* (March 27, 1740) with St. Paul's definition of charity (I Corinthians XIII):

> This is that amiable quality, which, like the sun, gilds over all our other virtues; this it is, which enables us to pass through all the offices and stations of life with real merit. This only makes the dutiful son, the affectionate brother, the tender husband, the indulgent father, the kind master, the faithful friend, and the firm patriot. This makes us gentle without fear, humble without hopes, and charitable without ostentation, and extends the power, knowledge, strength, and riches of individuals to the good of the whole. It is (as Shakespeare calls it) the milk, or rather the cream of human nature, and whoever is possessed of this perfection should be pitied, not hated for the want of any other. Whereas all other virtues without some tincture of this, may be well called *splendida peccata*. . . .[68]

Fielding suggests the further relationship of this principle to the highest Christian virtue when he styles God "the best-natured being in the universe,"[69] and later observes that good nature is "that heavenly frame of soul, of which Jesus Christ Himself was the most perfect pattern."[70] This it is, as he remarks in *The Covent-Garden Journal*, No. 16 (February 25, 1752), that "adorns the human, and is essential to the Christian Character."[71] The practical identification of good nature with his favorite Christian virtue of charity, however, may best be seen if we recall that its characteristic is a disinterested, universal, and active altruism, described in *Tom Jones* as "an active principle" that "doth not content itself with knowledge or belief only"—"a certain relative quality, which is always busying itself without-doors, and seems as much interested in pursuing the good of others as its own."[72]

Yet, ultimately, good nature was not enough. Because the Christian revelation surpasses "the religion of nature and philosophy" as a moral imperative, and because the impetuosity of his own heart often betrays the good man, Fielding was careful not to assert the complete self-sufficiency of good nature. Tom Jones, we recall, must repent his indiscretions before he earns Fielding's final approval, and Captain Booth, though "a man of consummate good nature," is not wholly acceptable until he has been convinced of the higher truth of Christianity. Good nature, though it is the essential characteristic of Fielding's heroes, is finally subsumed within the larger, more exalted concept of Christian charity, which, for example, teaches that highest maxim of morality: "Forgive the acts of your enemies."[73] In *The Champion* (March 27, 1740) Fielding indicates the difference more explicitly:

As good-nature, which is the chief if not only quality in the mind of man in the least tending that way, doth not forbid the avenging an injury, Christianity hath taught us something beyond what the religion of nature and philosophy could arrive at; and consequently, that it is not as old as the creation, nor is revelation useless with regard to morality, if it had taught us no more than this excellent doctrine, which, if generally followed, would make mankind much happier, as well as better than they are.[74]

The distinction is fine—one of degree, perhaps, and not of kind—but it is crucial nonetheless.

Like the latitudinarians, Fielding acknowledged that charity was "so certain a Duty by the Law of Nature," but he insisted as well upon its distinctively Christian character, having been more clearly and expressly "enjoined by the divine Dispensation."[75] Nothing more markedly demonstrates his close affinity with the rational divines than the unchanging emphasis in his writings upon this —"the greatest Virtue in the World"[76]—as the supreme and indispensable obligation of every Christian. Charity, he declares in *The Champion* (February 16, 1739/40)

> ... is a truly Christian virtue, nay, I will venture to say, the most Christian virtue: it is this, which, in the Scripture language, "covers a multitude of sins"; without which, to speak with the tongues of men and angels, is but as sounding brass or a tinkling cymbal; without which, prophecy, knowledge and faith are represented as nothing.[77]

Toward the close of his career, it is pronounced "a Virtue which is in Scripture said *to wash away [man's] Sins*, and without which all his other good Deeds cannot render him acceptable in the Sight of his Creator and Redeemer."[78]

With the latitudinarians against "that very wise Writer Dr. Mandevil," Fielding places the motives to true charity in a selfless "disinterested Benevolence"—"that brotherly love and friendly disposition of mind which is everywhere taught in Scripture."[79] Charity might begin at home, as Mrs. Tow-wouse prefers to think, but the philanthropy of the good man, says Fielding quoting Barrow, extends "to mere Strangers, towards such who never did him any good, or can ever be able to do him any."[80] In general, good nature may be viewed as the energetic predisposition to charity, which is the end of morality; for Fielding's ethic, like that of the divines, is practical and social in temper and aim. In making an active benevolence a necessary qualification of the ideal clergyman, for example, Fielding glosses St. Paul:

> Secondly, "charity is kind;" or, as the Greek signifies, does good offices, behaves kindly; not confined to our wishes merely, but our actions, under which head I shall introduce liberality, a necessary qualification of any who would call himself a successor of Christ's disciples. By this virtue, which is generally called charity itself (and perhaps it is the chief part of it), is not meant the ostentatious giving a penny to a beggar in the street . . . as if charity was change for sixpence, but the relieving the wants and sufferings of one another to the utmost of our abilities. It is to be limited by our power, I say, only.[81]

In *Tom Jones* (II, 5) this insistence upon the translation of good wishes into deeds is disclosed in the exchange between the pious hypocrite, Captain Blifil, and Squire Allworthy. The Captain, "not a little suspected of an inclination to Methodism," attempts to prove "that the word charity in Scripture nowhere means beneficence or generosity," but consists merely in " 'the forming of a benevolent opinion of our brethren' " rather " 'than a pitiful distribution of alms.'" As his author's spokesman, Allworthy replies in defense of an active liberality, concluding that the highest form of charity is "'where, from a principle of benevolence and Christian love, we bestow on another what we really want ourselves; where, in order to lessen the distresses of another, we condescend to share some part of them, by giving what even our own necessities cannot well spare.'"[82]

As with the extreme Arminian theology of his favorite latitudinarians—Barrow, Tillotson, Clarke, and Hoadly—Fielding realistically implemented the social objectives of his morality by making an active charity the condition of salvation. Nowhere is the essential Pelagianism of his position more apparent than in the Lucianic allegory, *A Journey from this World to the Next*, a document particularly important for our purposes because probably written soon after the conclusion of *Joseph Andrews*. Fielding seems to have anticipated the accusations of those who charged him, as Arthur Murphy records, "with an intention to subvert the settled notions of mankind in philosophy and religion,"[83] for in the Preface of the *Miscellanies* he feared having to vindicate himself "from designing, in an allegory of this kind, to oppose any present system, or to erect a new one of my own."[84] Very probably the Pelagian content of the *Journey* irritated the more orthodox or Methodist among its readers, those who habitually denounced the rational divines as Socinian or worse; but the moral of the tale itself was simply a highly imaginative rendering of the latitudinarian position, which emphasized good works over faith and extended salvation to the sincere and virtuous heathen. At the threshold of Elysium, Minos' standard of judgment is clear: "No man enters that gate without charity." After rejecting a pharisaical rigorist, a virtuoso philosopher, a coquette, a negligent parson, and a prude, Minos admits the narrator (who bears a close resemblance to Fielding) for his good nature and charity:

> The judge then addressed himself to me, who little expected to pass this fiery trial. I confessed I had indulged myself very freely with wine and women in my youth, but had never done an injury to any man living, nor avoided an opportunity of doing good, that I pretended to very little virtue more than general philanthropy and private friendship.—I was proceeding when Minos bid me enter the gate, and not indulge myself with trumpeting forth my virtues.[85]

The whole account of the various incarnations of Julian the Apostate, whose several attempts to earn salvation by a good life occupy the major portion of the *Journey*, comprises, furthermore, a lengthy demonstration of Fielding's Pelagianism.[86]

Consonant with the latitudinarian doctrine of works, Fielding thus insists that redemption is the reward of an energetic charity only. Several statements in *The Covent-Garden Journal* make this apparent. He declares in No. 39 (May 16, 1752), for instance, that "a Person void of Charity, is unworthy the Appellation of a Christian; that he hath no Pretence to either Goodness or Justice, or even to the Character of Humanity; that he is in honest Truth, an Infidel, a Rogue, and a Monster, and ought to be expelled not only from the Society of Christians, but of Men."[87] In No. 29 (April 11, 1752), he explicitly affirms that "as to that glorious Reward, the only one indeed which is worthy of a wise man's Consideration, which will attend the good Man hereafter, nothing is more certain than that he who deserves it is sure of attaining it; and the more real Delight we take in doing Good, the more we seem to acquire of such Merit."[88] And in No. 44 (June 2, 1752), he admonishes that unless a man have charity, "all his other good Deeds cannot render him acceptable in the Sight of his Creator and Redeemer."[89] Echoing Parson Adams, the good-natured men of the novels—Heartfree, Jones, and Dr. Harrison—reiterate the doctrine of works to the chagrin of sanctified hypocrisy. Heartfree, for example, annoys the bigoted ordinary of Newgate by voicing "a wicked sentiment . . . which we, who are truly orthodox, will not pretend to justify, that he believed a sincere Turk would be saved."[90] Similarly, Thwackum, the Pharisee, indignantly reproves Square for encouraging Tom Jones in the heresy "that there was no merit in faith without works."[91] And, in discussing his views on benevolence, Dr. Harrison asks his elderly friend:

"Is Christianity a matter of bare theory, and not a rule for our practice?"

"Practical, undoubtedly; undoubtedly practical," cries the gentleman. "Your example might indeed have convinced me long ago that we ought to do good to every one."[92]

Throughout his career as novelist, Fielding, following the example of the latitudinarian hostility to Whitefield, directed much of his sharpest satire against "the pernicious principles of Methodism." Fielding's morality, centered as it was in principles of practical social amelioration, was staunchly opposed to the Antinomianism of the Evangelists. After incidental allusions in *The Champion* (April 5 and May 24, 1740) to the Trapp-Whitefield controversy, he vigorously began his ridicule of the new "sect" in *Shamela*. With the aid of Whitefield's sermons and his *Short Account of God's Dealings with the Reverend Mr. George Whitefield,* Fielding's artful heroine rationalizes her frequent fornication, and Parson Williams, her paramour, is made to preach upon the disputed text, *"Be not Righteous overmuch."* Into the character of Williams, as Sheridan Baker has pointed out, go all the popular accusations against the licentious doctrine of the Methodists—their alleged claims of a special dispensation of grace, exempting them from good works and excusing sinful self-indulgence since salvation is a matter of confidence, not performance. Thus Shamela relates the substance of Williams' casuistry:

> Well, on *Sunday* Parson *Williams* came, according to his Promise, and an excellent Sermon he preached; his Text was, *Be not Righteous overmuch*; and, indeed, he handled it in a very fine way; he shewed us that the Bible doth not require too much Goodness of us, and that People very often call things Goodness that are not so. That to go to Church, and to pray, and to sing Psalms, and to honour the Clergy, and to repent, is true Religion; and 'tis not doing good to one another, for that is one of the greatest Sins we can commit, when we don't do it for the sake of Religion. That those People who talk of Vartue and Morality, are the wickedest of all Persons. That 'tis not what we do, but what we believe, that must save us, and a great many other good Things; I wish I could remember them all.[93]

The attack on Methodism continues in *Tom Jones* (VIII, 8), when Jones and Partridge pause in their travels for refreshment at the Bell Inn. Part of Fielding's compliment to its master is to notice that, though Whitefield's brother, he was "absolutely untainted with the pernicious principles of Methodism, or of any other heretical sect." The innkeeper's wife was also "free from any Methodistical notions," though her escape had been narrow. She had formerly purchased a long hood "in order to attend the extraordinary emotions of the Spirit; but having found, during an experiment of three weeks, no emotions, she says, worth a farthing, she very wisely laid by her hood, and abandoned the sect."[94] Indeed, Fielding's enduring suspicion of the sect is felt again in *Tom Jones* (XVIII, 13) and in *Amelia* (I, 4), where Methodism is depicted as a convenient rationale for accomplished hypocrisy. Blifil, we recall, finally has followed the inclination of his father and "turned Methodist, in hopes of marrying a very rich widow of that sect."[95] And during his brief term in Bridewell, Captain Booth encounters the Methodist Cooper, who preaches the "cant" doctrine of grace versus works to him and ends by picking his pocket:

"As for crimes [says Cooper], they are human errors, and signify but little; nay, perhaps the worse a man is by nature the more room there is for grace. The spirit is active, and loves best to inhabit those minds where it may meet with the most work. Whatever your crime be, therefore, I would not have you despair, but rather rejoice at it; for perhaps it may be the means of your being called."[96]

Fielding naturally detested the Antinomian inclinations of Whitefield's theology. The tenets of natural depravity, enthusiasm, and salvation by faith and the imputed righteousness of Christ served, he felt, as a too comfortable rationalization for self-indulgence, and dangerously subverted public morality. As the antithesis of

A Study of *Joseph Andrews*

his own Pelagian notions, Methodism was the inevitable target of his satire and the perfect foil to set off the practical advantage of the benevolist ethic to society.

To recapitulate, then, Fielding's view of human nature generally coincided with that of the latitudinarians in its over-all optimism. Because of his belief in the theory of a predominant passion, as well as his Christian conception of man's weakness since the Fall, he recognized that true good nature is rare. With Isaac Barrow and his own Dr. Harrison, however, he affirmed that man was essentially *capable* of great goodness, if only he were assisted by the institutions of society and persuaded by the powerful incentives of religion to a proper use of his reason and will. On the other hand, the completely moral man, like the heroes of the novels, was by nature compassionate, selfless, and benevolent—his heart so open and innocent that its generous impulses needed, for his own sake and that of society, to be directed and controlled by reason. This man, the good-natured man, wanted no other inducement to morality than his own benevolent disposition. His love for humanity naturally expressed itself in acts of charity, the supreme virtue and the sum of religion. Without charity, faith and knowledge and ritual were dead and were insufficient to salvation.

VI

The Novel: Meaning and Structure

IN THE search for the antecedents of Fielding's technique in *Joseph Andrews*, we have most often looked to the work of those authors whom he expressly admired—to Homer's *Odyssey*, Scarron's *Roman comique*, Le Sage's *Gil Blas*, Marivaux's *Marianne* and *Le Paysan parvenu*, Fénelon's *Télémaque*, and especially Cervantes' *Don Quixote*. (The importance of *Pamela* in the genesis of the novel is, of course, assumed.) These books—with the exception of *Marianne*, which is closer to Richardson than to Fielding —do indeed furnish a useful background to Fielding's practice in *Joseph Andrews*. In *Gil Blas* and the *Roman comique* the humorous adventures along the road interest us in a general way as skillful examples of a conventional motif. The *Odyssey, Le Paysan parvenu,* and *Télémaque* afford closer analogues to plot and incident in Fielding's novel. Like Adams and Joseph, Odysseus journeys homeward despite obstacles. Jacob, another young man from the country, is introduced into Parisian society and encounters the blandishments of Mme. de Ferval. Telemachus travels in search of his father and, aided by the good counsel of his spiritual guide, Mentor, preserves his chastity despite the charms of Calypso and Eucharis. More obvious than any of these, the influence of Cervantes appears not only in the resemblance between Don Quixote

A Study of *Joseph Andrews*

and Parson Adams, but also in a number of similarities in manner and incident.[1]

But the discovery in preceding literature of occasional parallels to the characters and events in *Joseph Andrews* helps very little to explain the art of Fielding's novel, its high measure of architectonic sophistication. After reading some of the critics, one is left with the impression that *Joseph Andrews* is little more than a pastiche of the work of Fielding's predecessors, or, perhaps, a kind of beadstring of amusing episodes assembled at random. F. Homes Dudden remarks, for instance, that many of the adventures in the novel, "though entertaining in themselves, and serviceable for bringing out idiosyncrasies of character, have little bearing on the main action and contribute nothing to the denouement." He adds later:

Joseph Andrews is still, on the whole, a tale of the picaresque type. The plan was not clearly thought out from the start, but almost seems to have been evolved extempore as the author proceeded.[2]

Fielding was too much aware of the important principle of unity, "that Epic Regularity," to compose in any such haphazard fashion. As much as he admired *Don Quixote*, he regretted its diffuseness of structure. In this respect, at least, he could prefer Charlotte Lennox's *Female Quixote* to its original: "Here is a regular Story, which, tho' possibly it is not pursued with that Epic Regularity which would give it the Name of an Action, comes much nearer to that Perfection than the loose unconnected Adventures in Don Quixote; of which you may transverse the Order as you please, without any Injury to the whole."[3] Earlier, in the Preface to his sister's

The Novel: Meaning and Structure

David Simple (1744), he implied that the ultimate formal model for *Joseph Andrews* was the *Odyssey*; this kind of writing, he observed, "consists of a series of separate adventures, detached from and independent on each other, yet *all tending to one great end,*" and for this reason it may not be criticized for "want of unity of action."[4] The concept of artistic unity that informs these remarks is more precisely defined in *Joseph Andrews* in an important, but neglected, passage. During his analysis of the *Iliad*, Parson Adams calls particular attention to a critical principle which he terms *Harmotton*, the correlation of structure and meaning; he asks:

"Is it possible for the Mind of Man to conceive an Idea of such perfect Unity, and at the same time so replete with Greatness? And here I must observe, what I do not remember to have been noted by any, the Harmotton, that agreement of his Action to his Subject: for, as the Subject is Anger, how agreeable is his Action, which is War; from which every Incident arises and to which every Episode immediately relates." (III, 2)

Those who are too ready to quarrel with Fielding for his ignorance of our post-Coleridgean shibboleth of organic unity would be wiser to examine his work in the light of such passages as the above.

The failure to recognize the unity of *Joseph Andrews* may be explained by an apparent blindness to the shaping importance of Fielding's moral purpose. Aurélien Digeon's comment is typical: "*Joseph Andrews* abattait Richardson et la doctrine de la chasteté profitable, mais l'enseignement positif en était presque nul, et le bon Adams ne pouvait guère être proposé en exemple."[5] George Sherburn has

A Study of *Joseph Andrews*

rightly observed, however, that Fielding was "fundamentally a moralist" and "one of the most thoughtful of English novelists."[6] Instruction, not merely entertainment, was the ultimate motive behind his first novel, though there is as much hearty good humor in *Joseph Andrews* as in any other book in English.

Theme imparts both meaning and cohesiveness to the loosely strung adventures and episodes of Fielding's odyssey of the road. In adopting this technique—one that comprehends the devices of parable and allegory in correlating subject and action—Fielding was only following a commonplace of neoclassical epic theory. Le Bossu, his favorite critic among the moderns, thus defined the epic as "un discours inventé avec art, pour former les moeurs par des instructions déguisées sous les allégories d'une action importante";[7] and he established as a rule that the fable (the theme or moral) of the epic was primary, the action being designed to embody and exemplify the particular moral that the work as a whole was to inculcate. These principles, widely accepted in England,[8] are only a more elaborate way of putting what Parson Adams understood by the term *Harmotton,* the agreement of action to subject.

The characters and plot of *Joseph Andrews* mutually function to illustrate the dominant thematic motifs of the novel, namely, the exposure of vanity and hypocrisy in society, and the recommendation of their antithetical virtues—charity, chastity, and the classical ideal of life. The journey in *Joseph Andrews* is not a mere picaresque rambling, a device solely for the introduction of new adventures such as we find in the *Roman comique, Gil Blas,* or *Don Quixote.* The wayfaring of Fielding's heroes

The Novel: Meaning and Structure

is purposeful, a moral pilgrimage from the vanity and corruption of the Great City to the *relative* naturalness and simplicity of the country.[9] In this respect Fielding, despite the hilarity of his comedy and his mock heroics, reminds us more of Bunyan or Fénelon than of Scarron, Le Sage, or Cervantes.

The two heroes of *Joseph Andrews,* furthermore, are more than merely a prudish young footman and a naïve parson. They embody the essential virtues of the good man—chastity and good nature. In accord with the preference for Christian heroes found both in the tradition of the biblical epic and in the homilies (especially Barrow's "Of Being Imitators of Christ"), the careers of Joseph Andrews and Abraham Adams comprise brilliantly comic analogues to those of their Scriptural namesakes, likewise patterns, according to the divines, of the good man's basic virtues. Joseph chastely resists the charms of his mistress and is at last reunited with the father from whom he had been kidnapped as a child. Brandishing his crabstick like a pilgrim's staff, Adams, the good patriarch and priest, travels homeward through strange and idolatrous countries, and is "tempted" by the near drowning of his son. The use of biblical analogues here, like the adaptation of the *Aeneid* in *Amelia,*[10] is surprisingly subtle, contributing to the mock-heroic character of the novel while at the same time reminding readers of the function of Joseph and Adams as exemplars. Finally, Adams as the true Christian minister has a more specific role in Fielding's efforts to correct a growing popular contempt of the clergy.

Again, I do not mean to suggest by these remarks and those that follow that Fielding was writing, not a great comic novel after all, but rather a book of Christian apologetics that now and then stoops to laughter. Fielding's good humor fills every page of *Joseph Andrews,* and we would be cheerless souls indeed who could not respond to it. But laughter and morality, as Fielding used to insist, are not incompatible. In *The Covent-Garden Journal,* No. 18 (March 3, 1752), he in fact spoke out against those who reject this proposition, who deny that wit and humor can be meant in earnest. His own practice is a case in point. As satirist, Fielding wrote both with a respect for his craft and with a sense of responsibility for the manners and morals of his age.

As we have already remarked, the theme of *Joseph Andrews* is implicit in its structure, the symbolic pilgrimage of its good men from the Great City to Parson Adams' country parish. For its titular hero the movement of the novel is, in effect, a quest to regain a rural paradise lost after the arrival in London. This motif is developed with more scope and sophistication, if less logically, in *Tom Jones.* After Tom is expelled from Squire Allworthy's significantly named Paradise Hall, for example, Fielding pointedly alludes to Milton's epic:

> And now having taken a resolution to leave the country, he began to debate with himself whither he should go. The world, as Milton phrases it, lay all before him; and Jones, no more than Adam, had any man to whom he might resort for comfort or assistance.[11]

Before he may resume his country idyll, with his nature "corrected by continual conversation with this good man [i.e., Allworthy], and by his union with the lovely and virtuous Sophia,"[12] and with Parson Adams replacing

Thwackum as spiritual counselor, Jones must come of age morally by profiting from his indiscretions in the great world. Similarly Joseph Andrews, "now in the one and twentieth Year of his Age" and under the guidance of his spiritual father Abraham Adams, reaches moral maturity, as did Mr. Wilson, by fleeing from the vitiating pressures of the town to seek, in a better country, union and happiness with a chaste and loving wife.[13] Although we are not dealing with the elaborate and detailed systems of Dante or Spenser or Bunyan, the reinforcement of meaning by action here adds the further dimension of allegory—broad and rudimentary, yet nonetheless thematically significant—to this hearty novel of the highway.

For Fielding, town and country were always morally antithetical. They tended, respectively, to acquire values symbolic of the extremes of worldly vanity and vice, and true virtue and contentment. As Professor Sherburn has noticed, "Whenever he writes about London his tone becomes grim, hard, distressing."[14] For example, Wisemore, the hero of Fielding's earliest play, *Love in Several Masques* (1728), remarks that "London would seduce a saint";[15] and Jack Commons in *The Letter Writers* (1731) refers to the city as "the charming plains of iniquity," a "delicious lewd place" that will be the inspiration for one final debauch.[16] Later, at the height of his career as novelist and magistrate, Fielding concentrated his stored-up resentment against the luxury, immorality, and irreligion of London into the sternly hortatory pages of *A Charge to the Grand Jury* (1749). Using a figure familiar to critics of pastoral poetry, he sometimes referred to the moral decadence of contemporary high society as characteristic of "this Gothic leaden age,"[17] and contrasted his own times with the simplicity and naturalness of "the first Ages of the World."[18] After depicting the corruption of country innocence in *Miss Lucy in Town* (1742), Fielding has his heroine speak an epilogue:

> Welcome again, ye rural plains;
> Innocent nymphs and virtuous swains:
> Farewell town, and all its sights;
> Beaus and lords, and gay delights:
>   All is idle pomp and noise;
>   Virtuous love gives greater joys.

In the country, Lucy's husband had declared, "there is still something of Old England remaining."[19]

Fielding's preference for the country, of course, was not the product of any foolish idealism about the absence of vice in a rural setting. He was not so naïve as that. Ambition and vanity, he remarked in *Tom Jones* (IV, 7), "flourish as notably in a country church and churchyard as in the drawing-room or in the closet,"[20] and his point is abundantly made in the novels by a host of selfish and hypocritical country squires, innkeepers, justices, and parsons. But, although human nature is essentially the same everywhere, Fielding did feel that in the country it is found in a "more plain and simple manner," without "all the high French and Italian seasoning of affectation and vice which courts and cities afford."[21] What is more, in the country a man could breathe the natural air and attend to the basic values of life, free from the toxic pressures of the town. Accordingly, Fielding's antidote for the city is the familiar classical ideal of rural retirement with a virtuous and loving wife. This is the solution recommended in all the novels and adopted by Tom Jones

The Novel: Meaning and Structure

and Sophia, Booth and Amelia, Joseph Andrews and Fanny, and, pre-eminently, the Wilsons.[22] In *Amelia* (III, 12) Dr. Harrison calls his plain country home "his earthly paradise," and advises Booth and Amelia to pursue "a country life." When supplemented by the fuller accounts of Wilson's mode of life and that of the clergyman depicted in *The Champion* (February 26, 1739/40), Booth's representation of the perfect contentment he and Amelia knew on the farm provides a good summary of his author's position:

"I scarce know a circumstance that distinguished one day from another. The whole was one continued series of love, health, and tranquillity. Our lives resembled a calm sea——"

". . . who can describe the pleasures which the morning air gives to one in perfect health; the flow of spirits which springs up from exercise; the delights which parents feel from the prattle and innocent follies of their children; the joy with which the tender smile of a wife inspires a husband; or lastly, the cheerful, solid comfort which a fond couple enjoy in each other's conversation? All these pleasures and every other of which our situation was capable we tasted in the highest degree."[23]

In *Joseph Andrews* this conventional symbolic polarity of city versus country most evidently informs the Wilson episode, which comprises the philosophical core of the novel, but it functions as well in the process of Joseph Andrews' education. Fortified by Adams' "many Admonitions concerning the Regulation of his future Conduct, and his Perseverance in Innocence and Industry" (I, 3), Joseph could withstand the solicitations of his Mrs. Potiphar and preserve his chastity even in the hostile environment of Mayfair. But while "his Morals remained entirely uncorrupted" (I, 4), the innocence and simplicity of his manners were at once tainted, much to the delight of Lady Booby, by exposure to the vanities of London: "She plainly saw the Effects which the Town-Air hath on the soberest Constitutions." Encouraged by "his party-coloured Brethren, who endeavoured to make him despise his former Course of Life," Joseph affected the latest fashions, led the opinion of the footmen at the opera and their rioting at the playhouses, and—clearest sign of the danger of a more serious moral aberration — seldom attended church, where "he behaved with less seeming Devotion than formerly." Assisted, however, by Adams' "good Advice and good Example" (I, 10), Joseph resists temptation and recognizes the thorough degeneracy of "the great City," which the good parson, following his namesake, later compares to Sodom,[24] and where the highest precept of morality goes unobserved. "London is a bad Place," Joseph writes to Pamela, "and there is so little good Fellowship, that next-door Neighbours don't know one another" (I, 6). The flight from London, its affectation and fornication, toward reunion in the country with Adams[25] and Fanny thus acquires, especially after the establishment of the classical ideal in the Wilson episode (III, 4), broadly allegorical connotations. To use the language of the homilies, it is a moral pilgrimage through a world of vanity and vexation to a better country.

The major thematic motif of *Joseph Andrews*, the doctrine of charity, principally informs Part II of the novel (Book I, chapter 11, through Book III), containing the adventures on the road and dominated, appropriately enough, by the figure of the good patriarch and priest, Abraham Adams. The theme of Christian charity is sounded at the start of Joseph's journey by the dramatic recasting of the Good Samaritan parable. Though the episode (I, 12) is often adduced as an example of Fielding's hearty humanitarianism, its specific thematic implications have not been explored. The parable of the Good Samaritan (Luke X: 25-37)—prompted by the lawyer's questions, "What shall I do to inherit eternal life?" and "Who is my neighbour?"—was frequently cited by such divines as Benjamin Hoadly as inculcating "the great Duty of universal Charity, and a most comprehensive Compassion."[26] This also is the Pelagian message of *Joseph Andrews*, which asserts that salvation is the reward of an active, universal benevolence. The account of Joseph's falling among the thieves in his passage from London is meant, quite deliberately, to recall both the parable and its Christian message. At the outset of his pilgrimage Fielding's hero is literally thrown naked upon the world. Robbed, beaten, stripped, and left for dead by the roadside, Joseph is grudgingly rescued by the self-interested passengers of the stage and given lodgings at the Dragon Inn. His only real comfort, however, comes from the Samaritan offices of two social outcasts, a postilion "since transported for robbing a Henroost" and a chambermaid, who clothe his nakedness in a traditional gesture of charity.[27] The dramatic enactment of this parable of Christian benevolence is a perfect introduction to the dominant ethical theme of the novel.

The concept of charity presented in *Joseph Andrews* is the inevitable outgrowth of Fielding's latitudinarian sympathies. That Parson Adams, his author's spokesman, stands squarely with the Pelagian doctrines of the liberal divines—and especially with Fielding's admired friend

A Study of *Joseph Andrews*

Benjamin Hoadly—is most apparent from his vigorous criticism of Whitefield and of the High Church denigration of Hoadly's *A Plain Account of the Nature and End of the Sacrament of the Lord's Supper* (I, 17). Against Barnabas, a self-indulgent, pleasure-loving High Churchman, Adams concurs with Whitefield's efforts to restore the Church "to the Example of the Primitive Ages." He is, however, equally opposed to the Antinomian tendencies of the popular Methodist, whose tenets he finds dangerously subversive of the highest sanctions of social morality:

"When he began to call Nonsense and Enthusiasm to his Aid, and to set up the detestable Doctrine of Faith against good Works, I was his Friend no longer; for surely that Doctrine was coined in Hell; and one would think none but the Devil himself could have the Confidence to preach it. For can anything be more derogatory to the Honour of God than for Men to imagine that the All-Wise Being will hereafter say to the Good and Virtuous, 'Notwithstanding the Purity of thy Life, notwithstanding that constant rule of Virtue and Goodness in which you walked upon Earth, still, as thou didst not believe everything in the true Orthodox manner, thy want of Faith shall condemn thee?' Or, on the other side, can any doctrine have a more pernicious Influence on Society, than a persuasion that it will be a good Plea for the Villain at the last day—'Lord, it is true I never obeyed one of thy Commandments, yet punish me not, for I believe them all?' "—"I suppose, sir," said the Bookseller, "your sermons are of a different kind."—"Aye, Sir," said Adams; "the contrary, I thank Heaven, is inculcated in almost every Page, or I should belye my own Opinion, which hath always been, that a virtuous and good Turk, or Heathen, are more acceptable in the sight of their Creator than a vicious and wicked Christian, though his Faith was as perfectly Orthodox as St. Paul himself." (I, 17)

The Novel: Meaning and Structure

Into the good parson's diatribe went virtually the sum and substance of latitudinarian antagonism to Whitefield; his was a comfortable and licentious doctrine, a convenient rationale for hypocrisy, and, above all, a doctrine pernicious to society, making salvation a matter of credulity and confidence rather than the practical exercise of virtue and charity. Adams, in apparent paraphrase of Hoadly's "The Good Samaritan,"[28] believed that salvation was offered to all men, infidels as well as believers, upon the conditions of sincerity and good works.

For similar reasons Adams endorsed Hoadly's rationalistic conception of the eucharist against his more orthodox opponents, among them the pompous, punch-drinking parson Barnabas. These opponents Adams includes, rather unfairly, in the ranks of those "few designing factious Men, who have it at heart to establish some favourite Schemes at the Price of the Liberty of Mankind, and the very Essence of Religion." Hoadly's mystery-dispelling account of the sacrament as a simple communal memorial of Christ's sacrifice, a time for recognizing one's fellowship with the body of Christians and for dedicating one's life to "The Uniform Practice of *Morality*,"[29] receives Adams' warmest praise:

"Witness that excellent Book called, 'A Plain Account of the Nature and End of the Sacrament;' a book written (if I may venture on the Expression) with the Pen of an Angel, and calculated to restore the true Use of Christianity, and of that Sacred Institution; for what could tend more to the noble Purposes of Religion than frequent chearful Meetings among the Members of a Society, in which they should, in the Presence of one another, and in the Service of the Supreme Being, make Promises of being good, friendly, and benevolent to each other?" (I, 17).

A Study of *Joseph Andrews*

Adams' recommendation of this controversial tract is in accord with the liberal Christianity of his author, who had lamented in *The Champion* (March 15, 1739/40) that "Religion and laws have been adulterated with so many needless and impertinent ceremonies, that they have been too often drawn into doubt and obscurity."[30] His advocacy of a common-sense religion of practical morality against the principles of Methodism and the High Church places him directly in the latitudinarian tradition.

From Adams' frequent discussions of charity there emerges a definition of the concept that corresponds precisely to that of the liberal divines examined earlier. True charity, which merits salvation, is not a matter of mere knowledge or profession or inclination, nor is it that self-centered, mercenary generosity cynically described by Hobbes and Mandeville. Rather, it is rooted in a good-natured, disinterested compassion, actively relieving the distresses and promoting the welfare of mankind. Fielding's satire of the Hobbesian man, whose altruism is constrained and selfishly motivated, is clearly implied in the "Good Samaritan" episode. By persuading the other passengers of the stage that Joseph must be rescued lest they be held legally responsible for his death, the lawyer—a "mean selfish Creature . . . who made Self the Centre of the whole Creation, would give himself no Pain, incur no Danger, advance no Money, to assist or preserve his Fellow-Creatures" (III, 1) — perfectly exemplifies the moral worthlessness of a merely politic philanthropy. Similarly inadmissible is the self-interested charity of Mrs. Tow-wouse, who extends hospitality to Joseph only when she believes he can afford it (I, 15), or of Mrs. Slipslop, who discharges Joseph's debt so that he will be a more accessible target for her lust (II, 3). This is that Mandevillean charity that Fielding later explicitly condemns in *The Covent-Garden Journal,* No. 21 (March 14, 1752), and which he here traces to Vanity (or self-love): "O Vanity! . . . Sometimes thou dost wear the Face of Pity, sometimes of Generosity" (I, 15). "Now true Charity," as Adams remarks in a letter to *The True Patriot,* No. 7 (December 17, 1745), "is of another kind, it has no self-interested Motives, pursues no immediate Return nor worldly Good, well knowing that it is laying up a much surer and much greater Reward for itself."

Nor does true charity, of the kind necessary to salvation, consist in knowledge or profession only. Adams' "Embassy" to the niggardly, porcine parson Trulliber underscores the requirement of action. Like the letter-learned Pharisees he typifies, Trulliber is well versed in Scripture and quick to mouth *contemptus mundi* platitudes paraphrased from the New Testament. For him, however, charity is a matter for speculation only, not performance, and the pearls of Pelagian good counsel that Adams casts before him go unheeded:

"I am sorry," answered Adams, "that you do know what Charity is, since you practise it no better: I must tell you, if you trust to your Knowledge for your Justification, you will find yourself deceived, though you should add Faith to it, without good Works." "Fellow," cries Trulliber, "dost thou speak against Faith in my House? Get out of my Doors: I will no longer remain under the same Roof with a Wretch who speaks wantonly of Faith and the Scriptures." "Name not the Scriptures," says Adams. "How! not name the Scriptures! Do you disbelieve the Scriptures?" cries Trulliber. "No; but you do," answered Adams "if I may reason from your Practice; for their Commands are so explicit, and their Rewards and Punishments so immense, that it is impossible a Man should stedfastly believe without obeying. Now, there is no Command more express, no Duty more frequently enjoined, than Charity. Whoever, therefore, is void of Charity, I make no scruple of pronouncing that he is no Christian." (II, 14)

Later, in *The True Patriot,* No. 7 (December 17, 1745), Adams repeats this final admonition, reasserting the supreme importance of "that Virtue without which no Man can be a Christian, namely Charity." Trulliber's brand of sanctified hypocrisy, furthermore, makes him nearly allied to another character, the false promiser, whose easy professions of future benefactions, by raising unfulfilled expectations, bring ruin and disgrace to those he pretends to oblige (II, 16-17).[31]

True charity, then, is both disinterested and energetic, rooted in the good-natured social affections. "A generous Disposition to relieve the distressed" (III, 13) is Adams' partial rendering of a definition given in Isaac Barrow's "The Duty and Reward of Bounty to the Poor." (To allow the miser Peter Pounce to betray himself, Adams' version omits the further requirement that "we should really express that disposition in our practice.")[32] Like Captain Blifil in *Tom Jones* (II, 5), Peter Pounce chooses to misconstrue the sense of his text: " 'There is something in that Definition,' answered Peter, 'which I like well enough; it is, as you say, a Disposition, and does not so much consist in the Act as in the Disposition to do it.' " Good works, an active charity, however, was the criterion for Adams' criticism of both Whitefield and Trulliber, and he revealed his own rule of conduct when he declared to the itinerant Catholic priest: "Sir . . . if I had the greatest Sum in the

World—aye, if I had ten Pounds about me—I would bestow it all to rescue any Christian from Distress" (III, 8). Earlier, upon arrival at the Dragon Inn, he had advised the surgeon attending Joseph that " 'it was the duty of Men of all Professions to apply their Skill *gratis* for the Relief of the Poor and Necessitous' " (I, 14), a sentiment Fielding elaborated in *The Covent-Garden Journal*, No. 29 (April 11, 1752), in declaring that an active charity need not be limited to almsgiving.

The distinctively Christian character of this virtue, furthermore, is indicated by the obligation to extend its energies even to the forgiveness of injuries. "Forgive the acts of your enemies hath been thought the highest maxim of morality," Fielding wrote in *An Essay on the Knowledge of the Characters of Men,* and he asserted in *The Champion* (March 27, 1740) that this exalted Christian precept surpassed the instinctive altruism of simple good nature. Despite his integrity and goodness, Joseph Andrews, under the incompetent guidance of parson Barnabas, is unable to attain that pitch of charity. Advised by Barnabas to forgive the thieves who had robbed and beaten him, Joseph answered:

'He feared that was more than he could do; for nothing would give him more Pleasure than to hear they were taken.'—"That," cries Barnabas, "is for the sake of Justice."—"Yes," said Joseph, "but if I was to meet them again, I am afraid I should attack them, and kill them too, if I could."—"Doubtless," answered Barnabas, "it is lawful to kill a Thief; but can you say you forgive them as a Christian ought?" Joseph desired to know what that forgiveness was. "That is," answered Barnabas, "to forgive them as—as—it is to forgive them as—in short, it is to forgive them as a Christian." Joseph replied, 'He forgave them as much as he could.'—"Well, well," said Barnabas, "that will do." (I, 13)

Unlike Barnabas, Adams, the authentic clergyman, insists upon the performance of this Christian obligation. Dueling and imprisonment for debt were for Adams, as well as for Fielding, egregious violations of this duty. The good parson is quick to censure the conduct of the elderly gentleman who, "out of pure Charity," offered to arrange a duel between Mr. Wilson and a captain of the guards (III, 3), and he speaks out vehemently against the tailor who had Wilson committed to prison for being unable to discharge his account:

"He may expect Mercy," cries Adams, starting from his Chair, "where he will find none! How can such a Wretch repeat the Lord's Prayer; where the Word, which is translated, I know not for what Reason, 'Trespasses,' is in the Original, 'Debts'? And as surely as we do not forgive others their Debts, when they are unable to pay them, so surely shall we ourselves be unforgiven when we are in no Condition of paying." (III, 3)

Like Isaac Barrow, whose discourse "Of Being Imitators of Christ" apparently influenced Fielding's choice of hero and situation, Joseph Andrews suggests a further extension of the meaning of charity in the novel when he argues, at some length, that true honor is the reward only of an active benevolence (III, 6).[33] This, too, is the lesson imparted in the Preface to the *Miscellanies*, where Fielding distinguishes between the Great and the Good preparatory to his characterization of Jonathan Wild and Heartfree. If we except the sustained irony of Wild's portrayal, the heroes of the novels are uniformly men of good nature and charity; they are, in the sense of Steele and the homilists, Christian heroes. Greatness, on the other hand, if reduced to its essential components of self-love and duplicity, is simply another expression of the Ridiculous, the object of Fielding's satire. As his metaphor of "the Ladder of Dependence" illustrates, it is not confined to high society, but descends to the meanest manifestations of vanity, "so that to a Philosopher the Question might only seem, whether you would choose to be a great Man at six in the Morning, or at two in the Afternoon" (II, 13). Whatever his station, the "great" man deserves the satirist's corrective lash.

But the man of charity is truly honorable; he is heroic for virtue's sake. And this is so even if in his ardent pursuit of the good his simplicity sometimes makes us smile. An important limitation in Fielding's theory of the Ridiculous is that it is an account of *satiric* laughter only; as Arthur Murphy long ago pointed out, it does not explain the pure, warm-hearted *comedy* of Parson Adams.[34] We must be careful to distinguish between the simply comic aspects of Fielding's good men and the Ridiculous, which is the target for exposure and correction. "I defy the wisest Man in the World," says Joseph Andrews, "to turn a true good Action into Ridicule" (III, 6). Adams' innocence or Joseph's militant chastity may excite laughter, but never the moral castigation and contempt implicit in Fielding's definition of the Ridiculous,[35] which consists principally in the deviation from "the most golden of all Rules, no less than that *of doing to all Men as you would they should do unto you*"—the deviation, in other words, from the rules of charity and good breeding.[36] A lack of charity, indeed, is the criterion of the Ridiculous. It is remarkable how often Fielding's satiric method is to oppose, in a given situation, the selfish and social passions and to direct our critical laughter against those whose avarice or lust or ambition or vanity subdues the requirements of compassion. Although expressed more subtly, or not openly expressed at all, the sentiments of the satirized in Fielding's novels may be finally reduced to Mrs. Tow-wouse's exclamation—"Common charity, a f——t!" (I, 12). In *Joseph Andrews,* Fielding's Christian heroes, patterns of the comprehensive virtues of chastity and charity, constitute, like the *vir bonus* of classical satire, a salutary alternative to this controlling satiric motif.

Behind the conception of Parson Adams in his capacity as exemplar—his origin in fiction must be traced to Don Quixote—lies the whole homiletic tradition of the good man, whose biblical prototype, it will be recalled, was Abraham—father of the faithful, whose faith was proved (according to St. James) by good works; a pilgrim "adhering stedfastly to the *True Religion,* in the *midst* of idolatrous and corrupt Nations."[37] Adams' name, character, and vocation, for example, combine Samuel Clarke's two examples of the good man, the patriarch Abraham and the true clergyman. And, with due acknowledgment of the bathetic adaptation of the epic in *Joseph Andrews,* Fielding's Christian hero as militant champion of truth and innocence ingeniously conforms to contemporary theories of the biblical epic and, in particular, to Isaac Barrow's preference for the "lives and examples of holy men" over the imaginary exploits of pagan heroes.

After his charity and goodness of heart, perhaps the most meaningful aspect of Adams' character as exemplar is his embodiment of Fielding's ideal of the true clergyman. As we shall see, it was a persistent aim of Fielding's writings both to rectify a widespread contempt of the clergy and to reform by ridicule the flagrant abuses within the Church that were the causes of that contempt. The "Apology for the Clergy," appearing in four numbers of *The Champion* (March 29, April 5, 12, and 19, 1740), is an important indication that the representation of Adams in contrast to Barnabas, Trulliber, and the other ignorant, pleasure-loving, hypocritical parsons of *Joseph Andrews* was prompted by precisely these reforming motives. For the moral health of society, Fielding felt, competent and dedicated clergymen and educators were indispensable. The office of the clergy, as successors to the disciples of Christ, was of final importance: "To call or summon men into the kingdom of God, and by spreading the excellence of His doctrine to induce men to become followers of Christ, and by that means partakers of His salvation."[38] They are "to point out and lead men into the ways of virtue and holiness by the frequent admonition of their precepts, and the constant guide of their examples."[39] In the final number of this series, Fielding defined the true clergyman as the supremely good man; the portrait stands as a kind of preliminary conceptual study of Parson Adams:

A clergyman is a successor of Christ's disciples: a character which not only includes an idea of all the moral virtues, such as temperance, charity, patience, &c. but he must be humble, charitable, benevolent, void of envy, void of pride, void of vanity, void of rapaciousness, gentle, candid, truly sorry for the sins and misfortunes of men, and rejoicing in their virtue and happiness. This good man is entrusted with the care of our souls, over which he is to watch as a shepherd for his sheep: to feed the rich with precept and example, and the poor with meat also. To live in daily communication with his flock, and chiefly with those who want him most (as the poor and distressed), nay, and after his blessed Master's example, to eat with publicans and sinners; but with a view of reclaiming them by his admonitions, not of fattening himself by their dainties.[40]

The opening paragraphs of *Joseph Andrews*, we will recall, establish the importance to society of the examples of good men, and the novel itself, by the dramatic expansion of a suggestion in Isaac Barrow's "Of Being Imitators of Christ," presents as heroes Abraham, father of the faithful, and Joseph, pattern of virtue. In confirmation of the ideal conception of the clergyman in *The Champion*, furthermore, Fielding's Preface explains the choice of Adams' profession: "No other office could have given him so many Opportunities of displaying his worthy Inclinations." The true pastor, whose function is ultimately social as well as religious, was pre-eminently in a position to shape and amend public morality. In describing a good clergyman and his family in *The Champion* (February 26, 1739/40), Fielding added that "the whole parish is by their example the family of love,"[41] and in *Amelia* (III, 12) Dr. Harrison's constant supervision and example have a similar effect on his parish. In *Joseph Andrews* the beneficial influence that Adams' good counsel and practice have exerted upon his cure further underscores the social function of the clergy. In contrast to the ill example of Trulliber, whose parishioners "all lived in the utmost Fear and Apprehension of him" and imitated his uncharitableness (II, 15), Adams' benevolence and careful attention to the spiritual needs of his community produce fruits of charity (II, 15) and discipline rooted in love: "Indeed his Word was little less than a Law in his Parish; for as he had shown his Parishioners, by a uniform Behaviour of thirty-five Years' duration, that he had their Good entirely at heart, so they consulted him on every Occasion, and very seldom acted contrary to his Opinion" (I, 11). Later, Fielding contrasts the joy inspired in Adams' parishioners by the return of Lady Booby and the parson:

> How much more forcibly did the Affection which they bore Parson Adams operate upon all who beheld his Return? They flocked about him like dutiful Children round an indulgent Parent, and vyed with each other in Demonstrations of Duty and Love. The Parson on his side shook every one by the Hand, inquiring heartily after the Healths of all that were absent, of their Children and Relations; and express a Satisfaction in his Face which nothing but Benevolence made happy by its Objects could infuse. (IV, 1)

In order to achieve this ultimate objective of social order, Fielding felt, the Christian minister must have a proper sense of the qualifications and obligations of his calling. "What fine things," exclaimed Joseph in gratitude to Adams for enabling him to triumph over temptation, "are good Advice and good Examples!" (I, 10). Heavily burdened with responsibility under the egregious pluralistic system—as curate "with a handsome Income of twenty-three Pounds a-Year" (I, 3), he must preach at four churches (II, 8)—Adams, with his author, shares Whitefield's devotion to the example of Primitive Christianity. In reproof of Barnabas he vigorously opposes the corruption of the superior clergy:

> "Sir," answered Adams, "if Mr. Whitefield had carried his Doctrine no farther than you mention, I should have remained, as I once was, his Well-Wisher. I am, myself, as great an Enemy to the Luxury and Splendour of the Clergy as he can be.

A Study of *Joseph Andrews*

I do not, more than he, by the flourishing Estate of the Church, understand the Palaces, Equipages, Dress, Furniture, rich Dainties, and vast Fortunes, of her Ministers. Surely those things, which savour so strongly of this World, become not the Servants of one who professed his Kingdom was not of it." (I, 17)[42]

In his subsequent dispute with the pragmatical alehouse-keeper, Adams—something of an anomaly in an age of widespread clerical ignorance, indolence, and luxury—proudly discloses his exalted conception of his office:

"There is something more necessary than Life itself, which is provided by Learning; I mean the Learning of the Clergy. Who clothes you with Piety, Meekness, Humility, Charity, Patience, and all the other Christian Virtues? Who feeds your Souls with the Milk of brotherly Love, and diets them with all the dainty Food of Holiness, which at once cleanses them of all impure carnal Affections, and fattens them with the truly rich Spirit of Grace [?]" (II, 17)

Spoken in the interest of the moral welfare of "his Children"—"He looked on all those whom God had entrusted to his Cure to stand to him in that Relation" (II, 16)—Adams' frequent exhortations to charity, patience, justice, truthfulness, and temperance, reinforced by the general conformity of his life, establish him indeed as a "valuable Pattern" of the Christian hero, wayfaring in a land of vanity and vexation. As a man and not a stiff and lifeless paragon like Dr. Harrison, his successor in *Amelia*, Adams has his weaknesses—such as his pride in his sermons (III, 3) and in his ability as a schoolmaster (III, 5)—but even these are the product of his idealism and dedication to the public welfare. And though the impractical side of his Christian Stoicism is amusingly revealed in the episode of his son's "drowning" (IV, 8), Adams' inability to follow his own advice on this occasion only sharpens our awareness of his compassionate nature. In a situation intentionally analogous to Abraham's resigned relinquishment of his son Isaac, Adams' paternal tenderness in this instance prevents his imitating the admired example of his namesake.[43]

In all other matters, however, where theory does not conflict with the generous impulses of his heart, Adams practices what he preaches. He is charitable (I, 15), forgiving (III, 7), hospitable (IV, 1), chaste (I, 10), truthful (II, 3), just in rewarding merit (II, 11), and courageous in defense of the weak and oppressed (II, 5, 9, and III, 9). As a true disciple of Christ, "who made no distinction, unless, peradventure, by preferring the Poor to the Rich" (III, 2), he benefits the penniless and distressed by his constant counsel and attendance. Although he concurs with Hoadly's attempts to purge the Church of its misconceptions concerning the nature and purpose of ritual, he is diligent in observing "the Forms of the Church" in the matter of marriage (II, 13); in this respect, Fielding's contemporaries would have contrasted him with the notorious parsons of the Fleet who, before the Marriage Act of 1753, made a profitable business of illegal marriages. He is no time-serving clergyman, but maintains his integrity despite intimidation from his superiors (II, 8, and IV, 2).[44] And remembering, perhaps, Chillingworth's celebrated declaration—"The Bible, I say, the Bible only, is the religion of the Protestants"—he is learned in the Scriptures to the point of emending the King James translation (III, 3, 8). Of nearly equal significance to his character as a clergyman, moreover, is his function as an educator: "He thought a Schoolmaster the greatest Character in the World" (III, 5). For, as we have already noticed, Fielding believed that much of the Ridiculous in society was owing to the prevalence of inadequate standards of education, promoting immorality by the indulgence of vanity and the encouragement of hypocrisy.

Joseph Andrews, and especially the character of Adams, is the first full dramatization of the concept of good nature that Fielding had enunciated in some detail in *The Champion* (March 27, 1740). There are moments in the novel when Fielding, like the school of sensibility, emphasizes the pleasurable transports of tenderness, pure and simple—as when, after her abduction, Fanny and Joseph are reunited: "O Reader! conceive if thou canst the Joy which fired the Breasts of these Lovers on this Meeting; and if thy own Heart doth not sympathetically assist thee in this Conception, I pity thee sincerely from my own; for let the hard-hearted Villain know this, that there is a Pleasure in a tender Sensation beyond any which he is capable of tasting" (III, 12); or when, upon their first meeting, Adams is shown "dancing about the Room in a Rapture of Joy . . . for the Goodness of his Heart enjoyed the Blessings which were exulting in the Breasts of both the other two, together with his own" (II, 12). Indeed, as Fielding later observes with reference to Captain Booth, tenderness and goodness are identical.[45] Joseph Andrews' greater concern on his "deathbed" for Fanny's grief than for his own danger (I, 13), or Fanny's compassion for the hare wantonly torn by the squire's dogs (III, 6), or Adams' openhearted gratitude to the pedlar who rescued his son (IV, 8), are random instances of this strain of sentimentalism in the novel. Fielding's primary criterion for true good nature, however, is its more palpable manifestation in an active social benevolence—that "generous Disposition to relieve the distressed" translated into deeds. Good nature in this sense is truly "that amiable quality, which, like the sun, gilds over all our other virtues."[46] The possession of this quality by one of Fielding's characters is an infallible indication of his author's sympathy. Like Tom Jones, for example, Betty the chambermaid's warm animal spirits render her chastity tenuous at best, but her "Good nature, Generosity, and Compassion" more than atone for her indiscretions; on the other hand, Mrs. Tow-wouse's self-interested insensibility to human misery deserves the castigation of Fielding's irony, "though she was as true to her Husband as the Dial to the Sun" (I, 18).

Of all Fielding's heroes, Parson Adams is the fullest personification of good nature. It is Adams' embodiment of the essential characteristics of this concept that permits Fielding to declare in his Preface—despite his hero's apparent likeness to Don Quixote[47]—that "the Character of Adams . . . is not to be found in any Book now extant." The theory of good nature formulated in *The Champion* provided an ethical, rather than literary, basis for Adams' distinctive traits: his compassion, charity, and, above all, his simplicity. Even his gravity of countenance (I, 14) may be traced to the empathic disposition of the good-natured man.[48] Instances of the "Goodness of his Heart" and "his worthy Inclinations" (Preface) are too frequent and obvious to require discussion here. Along with his moral idealism learned from the classics and primitive Christianity, however, the dominant feature of Adams' good nature, his simplicity, is consciously manipulated by Fielding to serve the ethical purpose of his satire. Adams, Fielding writes, was

... as entirely ignorant of the ways of this World as an Infant just entered into it could possibly be. As he had never any Intention to deceive, so he never suspected such a Design in others. He was generous, friendly, and brave to an Excess; but Simplicity was his Characteristic. (I, 3)

The "inoffensive Disposition of his own Heart" (III, 7) not only makes the parson slow to discover the impositions practiced upon him by the malicious and hypocritical, such as the false promiser or the confederates of the practical-joking squire—"a sort of People," writes Fielding with reference to Peter Pounce, "whom Mr. Adams never saw through" (III, 12)—but it also makes vivid by contrast the moral decadence and corruption of the world through which he moves. As revealed in *The Covent-Garden Journal*, No. 42 (May 26, 1752), an important but neglected essay on the *vanitas vanitatum* theme that locates the sources of the Ridiculous, Fielding conceives of Adams' innocence and idealism as an effective vehicle for exposing the folly and vice of society. Speaking here of the kind of scholar who derives his knowledge of the world from the classics rather than from experience—we may compare Adams' dispute with the widely traveled alehouse-keeper (II, 17)—he writes:

In solemn Truth, Gentlemen who obtain an early Acquaintance with the Manners and Customs of the Antients, are too apt to form their Ideas of their own Times, on the Patterns of Ages which bear not the least Resemblance to them. Hence they have fallen into the greatest Errors and Absurdities.[49]

The Novel: Meaning and Structure

He imagines "a Man, possessed of this Jaundice of Literature"—and, in Adams' case, we might add the jaundice of good nature—in his bewildered exposure to the vanities of the age: the levees of great men, country hunting matches and horse races, drums and routs, beaus and coquettes. We are reminded of Adams' amazed and outraged interpolations ("Good Lord! what wicked Times these are!") during Wilson's account of his rake's progress through London society: "A Scholar when he first comes to this Town from the University comes among a Set of People, as entirely unknown to him, and of whom he hath no more heard or read, than if he was to be at once translated into one of the Planets; *the World* in the Town and that *in the Moon* being equally strange to him, and equally unintelligible."[50] We may laugh at the parson's good-natured innocence and bookish idealism, but his honest bewilderment and shock at the great world imply a standard by which to measure the moral degeneracy of his age.

Pilgrim, priest, and patriarch, Abraham Adams maintains his faith in strange and idolatrous lands. Apparently following another of Barrow's suggestions, Fielding chose as his representative of chastity, symbolic of the rational discipline of the passions, a virtuous footman named Joseph, whose initial situation was not only sure to amuse by evoking the absurdities of *Pamela,* but was, in accord with the theories of the biblical epic, precisely parallel to the story of his "namesake" and Potiphar's wife.

This, of course, was an age of the "double standard," when, as Sarah Fielding's Miss Baden says in *The History of Ophelia,* chastity "was even made the Subject of Ridicule in such Men as were possessed of it,"[51] and it would

A Study of *Joseph Andrews*

be scarcely conceivable that the author of *Tom Jones* seriously undertook his first novel in defense of male chastity. Joseph's forcible expulsion of the warm-spirited Betty from his room at the Dragon Inn (I, 18) is certainly continence carried to a ludicrous extreme. "How ought Man to rejoice," Fielding facetiously comments, "that his Chastity is always in his own power; that, if he hath sufficient Strength of Mind, he hath always a competent Strength of Body to defend himself, and cannot, like a poor weak Woman, be ravished against his Will!" In *The Champion* (March 15, 1739/40) he had warned against allowing even "Virtue itself" to grow "too exuberant": "Men often become ridiculous . . . by over-acting even a laudable part."[52] And we have seen that Betty's good nature, like that of Tom Jones and the narrator of *A Journey from this World to the Next,* more than compensates for her indiscretions.

At the same time, however, it would be a mistake to underestimate the importance of chastity — even male chastity—in Fielding's morality. The "Character of Male-Chastity," he declares in the opening chapter of *Joseph Andrews,* is "doubtless as desirable and becoming in one Part of the human Species as in the other." Adultery, he feels, is "a Catastrophe, common enough, and comical enough too perhaps, in modern History, yet often fatal to the Repose and Well-being of Families, and the Subject of many Tragedies, both in Life and on the Stage" (I, 17). Although Betty's slip with Mr. Tow-wouse is a subject more for mirth than tears, the nearly tragic complications of Captain Booth's inconstancy pose a grave problem in *Amelia,* and even Tom Jones must repent and learn to discipline his passions before he is accepted by Sophia. In

The Novel: Meaning and Structure

The Covent-Garden Journal, No. 20 (March 10, 1752), Fielding's spokesman, the good-natured Axylus, regrets that the fashionable literature of the period has made adultery—"so execrable a Vice"[53]—seem a matter of jest and gallantry; and two later numbers of the *Journal,* Nos. 67 and 68 (October 21 and 28, 1752), urge the enactment of a law against it. Fielding says:

> I may venture, without apprehending the Imputation of Pedantry or Moroseness to encounter the present general Opinion, and to question whether Adultery be really that Matter of Jest and Fun which it is conceived to be, and whether it might not be decent and proper to contrive some small Punishment for this Vice in a civilized (much more in a Christian) Country.[54]

Twenty years earlier, Fielding had similarly criticized the loose marital standards of the day in his bitter comedy, *The Modern Husband* (1732). But perhaps his position with regard to male chastity is best shown in *The Wedding-Day* (1743), as Heartfort upbraids Millamour for his incontinence and defines his own attitude toward the double standard:

> My practice, perhaps, is not equal to my theory; but I pretend to sin with as little mischief as I can to others: and this I can lay my hand on my heart and affirm, that I never seduced a young woman to her own ruin, nor a married one to the misery of her husband....
>
> Custom may lead a man into many errors, but it justifies none; nor are any of its laws more absurd and unjust than those relating to the commerce between the sexes: for what can be more ridiculous than to make it infamous for women to grant what it is honourable for us to solicit, nay, to ensnare and almost compel them into; to make a whore a scandalous,

a whoremaster a reputable appellation! Whereas, in reality, there is no more mischievous character than a public debaucher of women."[55]

With regard to incontinence, as well as immorality in general, Fielding equally recognizes mitigating circumstances and motives; Captain Booth, for example, "though not absolutely a Joseph ... yet could ... not be guilty of premeditated inconstancy."[56] Upon occasion Fielding may excuse weakness in sexual matters, but he does not justify it. He stands squarely with Tom Jones, who remonstrates with Nightingale:

"Lookee, Mr. Nightingale," said Jones, "I am no canting hypocrite, nor do I pretend to the gift of chastity more than my neighbors. I have been guilty with women, I own it; but am not conscious that I have every [sic] injured any. Nor would I, to procure pleasure to myself, be knowingly the cause of misery to any human being."[57]

Joseph Andrews' chastity, however, has wider implications than merely the preservation of his virginity. Like their biblical prototypes, Abraham and Joseph, Fielding's good men exemplify the sum of the individual's duty to God, society, and himself. Adams' personification of true faith expressed through charity comprehends the first two and Joseph's chastity the last. Tillotson, we recall, had thus defined the head of our duty to ourselves: "That we govern our passions by reason, and moderate our selves in the use of sensual delights, so as not to transgress the rules of temperance and chastity." In *The Champion* for February 2, 1739/40, an essay of much interest in anticipating certain aspects of the characterization of Lady Booby, Fielding accordingly maintains the temperate ordering of the pas-

The Novel: Meaning and Structure

sions by reason and recommends the fulfillment of "that glorious precept *vince teipsum*":

> The conquest of one's self is justly preferred by wise men to that of armies and kingdoms. This is that courage which is so ardently recommended in our religion, and which, however passive it may be in regard to others, is extremely active with respect to one's self. Whoever carefully surveys his own mind, will find sufficient enemies to combat within; an army of obstinate passions that will hold him in tight play, will often force his reason to retreat; and if they are at length subdued, it will not be without much labour and resolution.[58]

At several points in *Joseph Andrews*, Fielding dramatizes this psychomachy in depicting the conflict between lust and hate and pride in the mind of the rejected Lady Booby (e.g., I, 9, and IV, 4, 13). Before learning that Joseph and Fanny may be brother and sister, for example, Lady Booby rationalizes her disappointment at their forthcoming marriage:

> "What am I doing? How do I suffer this Passion to creep imperceptibly upon me? . . . To sacrifice my Reputation, my Character, my Rank in Life, to the Indulgence of a mean and a vile Appetite! How I detest the Thought! How much more exquisite is the Pleasure resulting from the Reflection of Virtue and Prudence than the faint Relish of what flows from Vice and Folly! Whither did I suffer this improper, this mad Passion to hurry me, only by neglecting to summon the Aids of Reason to my Assistance?" (IV, 13)

Although throughout Joseph's second interview with Lady Booby, Fielding is poking fun at Pamela's ostentatious flaunting of her "virtue," the message of *vince teipsum*,

A Study of *Joseph Andrews*

more seriously presented in *The Champion,* plainly underlies the exchange:

"Would you be contented with a Kiss? [asks Lady Booby] Would not your Inclinations be all on fire rather by such a Favour?" "Madam," said Joseph, "if they were, I hope I should be able to controll them, without suffering them to get the better of my Virtue." (I, 8)

Assisted by the good advice and good example of Parson Adams—"(for he was a great Enemy to the Passions, and preached nothing more than the Conquest of them by Reason and Grace)" (IV, 8)—and inspired by his love for the chaste Fanny Goodwill, Joseph is able to resist the temptation of his Mrs. Potiphar. It would, of course, be absurd to suggest that Fielding's principal objective in describing Joseph's encounters with Lady Booby, Mrs. Slipslop, and Betty is not comedy, but the recommendation of a militant chastity. As with the innocence and idealism of Adams, Joseph's chastity is amusing because extreme; but it functions nonetheless as a wholesome antithesis to the fashionable lusts and intrigues of high society.

By now it should be clear that *Joseph Andrews* has from the start a surprisingly intricate design of its own—a pattern broadly allegorical, correlating theme and form and shaped by the Christian purpose of its author. But our analysis is not yet complete. Located at the heart of the book, the long biography of Mr. Wilson needs to be reckoned with.

Fielding, of course, had ample precedent for the insertion of "irrelevant" tales into the midst of his narrative. The practice was common to every narrator from Homer and Apuleius to Cervantes and Le Sage. In *Tom Jones* (V, 1), in fact, Fielding devised his own esthetic to defend the novelist's right to digress—"the art of contrast," he called it.[59] Unlike their modern detractors, Fielding and his fellow writers did not *over*value unity of structure; to them the principles of variety and contrast were equally appealing.[60] Yet we do an injustice to the complex craftsmanship of a skillful artist if we let the case for the Wilson episode rest here. It can be defended as well on grounds more congenial to our own times.

Most critics, however, look upon Wilson's story as another flaw—the most serious and glaring of all—in the random architecture of *Joseph Andrews*. F. Homes Dudden's objection that Fielding's digressions, and particularly the Wilson episode, "can hardly be justified on artistic grounds" is typical: "Wilson's history, indeed, comprises some matter relevant to the plot," he allows, "... but it would have been definitely an advantage had the greater part of it been omitted."[61] Admittedly, though they do lend the spice of variety to the narrative and though their themes of vanity and false love and marriage are pertinent to the novel as a whole, it is questionable whether the stories of Leonora (II, 4, 6) and Leonard and Paul (IV, 10) are worth the telling. Far from being a needless or irrelevant interpolation, however, the Wilson episode is essential. It stands as the philosophic, as well as structural, center of *Joseph Andrews*, comprising a kind of synecdochic epitome of the meaning and movement of the novel. Practically speaking as well, in a book whose satiric subject is vanity, provision had to be made for a long look at London, always for Fielding the symbol of *vanitas vanitatum*. Parson Adams, whose wayfaring is confined to the country, must be exposed to and permitted to comment on the affectations of the Great City. Wilson's story thus serves, economically, as a narrative version of what is dramatically, and therefore more effectively, presented in the final third of *Tom Jones*. *Joseph Andrews* represents the moral pilgrimage of its hero, guided by the good counsel and example of his spiritual father, Abraham Adams, from the folly and vice of London toward reunion in the country with the chaste and loving Fanny Goodwill. The digression focuses and moralizes this movement by depicting Wilson's progress—nearly disastrous because "without a Guide"—through the corrupting vanities of the town to a life of wisdom, love, and contentment in a setting reminiscent of the Golden Age. Under proper tutelage, Joseph has escaped the moral contamination of Wilson's London period and may profit from his hard-earned wisdom. The meaning of both the digression and the novel as a whole is largely a variation on the themes of Ecclesiastes, Juvenal's *Third Satire,* and Virgil's *Second Georgic,* controlled throughout, of course, by the doctrine of charity.

As an alternative to the immorality of the great world, Fielding early establishes the ideals of chaste love and marriage and a simple, useful life of retirement. The first half of this antithesis relates to a recurring motif in his writings, what A. R. Towers has called "a literary programme designed to glorify the pleasures of conjugal love"[62] and culminating in *Amelia*. For Fielding, "the two principal Female Characters [are] that of Wife, and that of Mother,"[63] and in the novels he embodies this ideal in Mrs. Wilson, Mrs. Heartfree, Amelia, and—by last-page implication—in Fanny and Sophia. In the fugitive poem "To a Friend on the Choice of a Wife," he defines his ideal at some length, and many of the features of this portrait reappear in the good women of the novels. A true wife, he feels, must attend to the useful domestic duties and must be a good-natured, sensible, and loving companion, yet willing to submit to the superior judgment of her husband. Speaking, perhaps, with the pattern of Charlotte Cradock in mind—"one from whom I draw all the solid comfort of my life"[64]—Fielding conceives of marriage to such a woman as a necessary ingredient of earthly contentment: "If fortune gives thee such a wife to meet, / Earth cannot make thy blessing more complete."[65] This is more effusively borne out by Letter XLIV, which Fielding contributed to his sister's *Familiar Letters between the Principal Characters in David Simple*:

> "Now, in my eye, [writes Valentine to Cynthia] love appears alone capable of bestowing on us this highest degree of human felicity. I solemnly declare, when I am in passion of my wife . . . my happiness wants no addition. I think I may aver, it could receive none. I conceive myself then to be the happiest of mankind. I am sure I am as happy as it is possible for me to be."[66]

Fielding's conception of the highest earthly happiness thus combines the ideas of chaste conjugal love and, as we have seen, a simple country life dissociated from the luxury, avarice, and ambition of the great world. This ideal, depicted in the account of Wilson's mode of life (III, 4), is first represented in *The Champion* (February 26, 1739/40) as Fielding contrasts the vanities of existence in the house of "a certain person of great distinction" with the quiet, affectionate, self-sufficient life of a country clergyman. "I am convinced," Fielding comments, "that happiness does not always sit on the pinnacle of power, or lie in a bed of state; but is rather to be found in that golden mean which Horace prescribes in the motto of my paper."[67]

But let us have a closer look at the Wilson episode and its place in the novel. On one level, what Fielding is attempting in the history of Mr. Wilson is a prose version of Hogarth's "progress" pieces. Specifically, the analogy between *The Rake's Progress* and Wilson's account of his London days is inescapable.[68] The reason for this parallelism is not hard to find. In the Preface to *Joseph Andrews* Fielding virtually identifies Hogarth's conception of the comic art and his own. Even more to the point, however, is his great admiration for the moral utility of his friend's satiric prints, especially, "the Rake's and the Harlot's Progress":

I esteem the ingenious Mr. Hogarth as one of the most useful satirists any age hath produced. In his excellent works you see the delusive scene exposed with all the force of humour, and, on casting your eyes on another picture, you behold the dreadful and fatal consequence. I almost dare affirm that those two works of his, which he calls the Rake's and the Harlot's Progress, are calculated more to serve the cause of virtue, and for the preservation of mankind, than all the folios of morality which have been ever written; and a sober family should no more be without them, than without the Whole Duty of Man in their house.[69]

Though the charity of Harriet Hearty saves him from Tom Rakewell's horrid end, the fictional tableau of Wilson's career as a beau and freethinker is a clear reflection of what Hogarth had done more graphically.

The Novel: Meaning and Structure

The story of Mr. Wilson, however, is much more than an imitation of Hogarth. Its function within the novel gives it a direction and complexity of its own. As with *Joseph Andrews* as a whole, vanity of vanities is the message of Wilson's progress through London society, his hard-earned wisdom through adversity, and his retirement to a life according to the classical ideal. Although Fielding's talent is not well suited to the novel of analysis, in its personal application Wilson's story is essentially one of moral education and regeneration of the type Fielding undertook in treating the predicament of Captain Booth in *Amelia*. While the emphasis throughout is on the exposure of fashionable folly and vice, Fielding is careful to suggest the moral dimension, tracing Wilson's spiritual degradation to its source in irreligion and a faulty education. Unlike Joseph Andrews, Wilson has not had the benefit of Parson Adams' good counsel: to his "early Introduction into Life, without a Guide," he remarks, "I impute all my future Misfortunes" (III, 3). Bad standards of education, Fielding later declares in two numbers of *The Covent-Garden Journal*, Nos. 42 and 56 (May 26 and July 25, 1752), are responsible for the prevalence of modern vanity and affectation; they are the true source of the Ridiculous. In *The True Patriot*, No. 13 (January 21-28, 1746), Parson Adams and Mr. Wilson, after observing the profligacy, francophilism, and irreligion of a young "Bowe," agree upon its causes. Adams' remarks pertain as well to Wilson's biography:

In discoursing upon this Subject, we imputed much of the present Profligacy to the notorious Want of Care in Parents in the Education of Youth, who, as my Friend informs me, with very little School Learning, and not at all instructed *(ne minime quidem imbuti)* in any Principles of Religion, Virtue and Morality, are brought to the Great City, or sent to travel to other Great Cities abroad, before they are twenty Years of Age; where they become their own Masters, and enervate both their Bodies and Minds with all Sorts of Diseases and Vices, before they are adult.

Wilson's spiritual impasse is also placed in a Christian context recalling the arguments for free will and the operation of Providence as against Fortune in Boethius' *Consolation of Philosophy* and the homilies. His brief flirtation with the "Rule-of-Right" club of deists and Hobbesian atheists is indicative of his state of mind. By blinding himself to the "Principles of Religion" and the operation of Providence, Wilson becomes caught up in the machinery of Fortune. "Prosperity" changes to "Adversity," and he sinks to a nadir of despair. Wilson's description of the principles of the club of deists and political philosophers to which he subscribed illustrates the nature of his problem:

These Gentlemen were engaged in a Search after Truth, in the Pursuit of which they threw aside all the Prejudices of Education, and governed themselves only by the infallible Guide of Human Reason. This great Guide, after having shown them the Falsehood of that very antient but simple Tenet, that there is such a Being as a Deity in the Universe, helped them to establish in His stead a certain "Rule of Right," by adhering to which they all arrived at the utmost Purity of Morals. Reflection made me as much delighted with this Society as it had taught me to despise and detest the former [i.e., a club of carousers]. I began now to esteem myself a Being of a higher Order than I had ever before conceived; and was the more charmed with this Rule of Right, as I really found in my own

Nature nothing repugnant to it. I held in utter Contempt all Persons who wanted any other inducement to Virtue besides her intrinsick Beauty and Excellence. (III, 3)

Wilson's disillusionment with "this delightful Dream" is occasioned by the inability of his philosopher companions to translate their theories into practice without the compelling incentives of religion. For the Christian precept of charity, they substituted their own inadequate imperative, and their immoral "Practices, so inconsistent with our golden Rule, made me begin to suspect its Infallibility." Breaking with this company and its principles, however, Wilson as yet could find no spiritually sustaining substitute: the society of poets he then frequents only proves to him the general prevalence of vanity, "the worst of Passions, and more apt to contaminate the Mind than any other"; it does not relieve his "State of Solitude."

The change from Wilson's "prosperous Days" begins when he, symbolically, becomes a "Gamester" and, trusting to Fortune and Chance instead of Providence, loses the rest of his inheritance:

This opened Scenes of Life hitherto unknown; Poverty and Distress, with their horrid Train of Duns, Attorneys, Bailiffs, haunted me Day and Night. My Clothes grew shabby, my Credit bad, my Friends and Acquaintance of all kinds cold. (III, 3)

After failing as playwright, hackney writer, and translator, Wilson, in a gesture significant of his spiritual blindness, "bought a Lottery-Ticket, resolving to throw myself into Fortune's Lap, and try if she would make me amends for the Injuries she had done me at the Gaming-Table."[70]

A Study of *Joseph Andrews*

The immediate result of his mistaken trust in Fortune is despair. Imprisoned for debt, he relates, "I had now neither Health . . . Liberty, Money, or Friends; and had abandoned all Hopes, and even the Desire, of Life." (Earlier in the narrative Adams had admonished him, "You should rather have thrown yourself on your knees . . . for despair is sinful.") Having disposed of his lottery ticket for a loaf of bread, he is plunged deeper into affliction by the news that he would have won three thousand pounds: "This was only a Trick of Fortune to sink me the deeper." And, like Job in his adversity, Wilson is deserted by his friends, one of whom, however, speaks with unconscious wisdom: "He said I was one whom Fortune could not save if she would." Languishing in prison like Boethius, and accusing Fortune of responsibility for his predicament, Wilson is rescued by the charity and love of his future wife and learns an important lesson. "Madam," he remarks to Harriet Hearty, "you mistake me if you imagine, as you seem, my Happiness is in the power of Fortune now." The moral is repeated as he smoothly corrects Parson Adams for an unfortunate figure of speech:

"Sir," says Adams, "Fortune hath, I think, paid you all her Debts in this sweet Retirement." Sir, replied the Gentleman, I am thankful to the great Author of all things for the Blessings I here enjoy. (III, 3)

Thus, having missed the benefits of good advice and good example, Wilson must earn his wisdom through the harsh discipline of adversity. As spiritual biography, his story dramatizes Fielding's recurrent insistence upon the operation of Providence and the moral responsibility of the individual. It is the same Boethian argument devel-

The Novel: Meaning and Structure

oped at greater length in *Amelia*. Fielding's introduction to the story of Captain Booth also has relevance to Mr. Wilson:

> I question much whether we may not, by natural means, account for the success of knaves, the calamities of fools, with all the miseries in which men of sense sometimes involve themselves, by quitting the directions of Prudence, and following the blind guidance of a predominant passion; in short, for all the ordinary phenomena which are imputed to fortune, whom perhaps, men accuse with no less absurdity in life than a bad player complains of ill luck at the game of chess.[71]

More important for the novel as a whole, however, is the apparent lesson to be drawn from Wilson's history: *vanitas vanitatum* and its solution in "a retired life" of love and simplicity.

> In short, [Wilson moralizes] I had sufficiently seen that the Pleasures of the World are chiefly Folly, and the Business of it mostly Knavery, and both nothing better than Vanity; the Men of Pleasure tearing one another to pieces from the Emulation of spending Money, and the Men of Business from Envy in getting it. My Happiness consisted entirely in my Wife, whom I loved with an inexpressible Fondness, which was perfectly returned; and my Prospects were no other than to provide for our growing Family; for she was now big of her second Child: I therefore took an Opportunity to ask her Opinion of entering into a retired life, which, after hearing my Reasons and perceiving my Affection for it, she readily embraced. We soon put our small Fortune, now reduced under three thousand Pounds, into Money, with part of which we purchased this little place, whither we retired soon after her Delivery, from a World full of Bustle, Noise, Hatred, Envy, and Ingratitude, to Ease, Quiet, and Love. (III, 3)

A Study of *Joseph Andrews*

In depicting the Wilsons' life of retirement, simplicity, industry, and mutual love, Fielding presents as a wholesome alternative to the corruption of the Great City the familiar classical ideal of the happy husbandman—"Vanity had no Votary in this little spot" (III, 4). He is careful, however, to make that compromise with complete detachment and solitude that the latitudinarian ethic of practical benevolence required. Wilson is no misanthropist or hermit such as the Man of the Hill; he is hospitable to his guests and, what especially pleases Adams, charitable to his neighbors:

These Instances pleased the well-disposed Mind of Adams equally with the Readiness which they exprest to oblige their Guests, and their Forwardness to offer them the best of everything in their House; and what delighted him still more was an Instance or two of their Charity; for whilst they were at Breakfast the good Woman was called for to assist her sick Neighbour, which she did with some Cordials made for the publick Use, and the good Man went into his Garden at the same time to supply another with something which he wanted thence, for they had nothing which, those who wanted it were not welcome to. (III, 4)

"This," declares Adams, "was the Manner in which the People had lived in the Golden Age." Indeed, there is a conscious flavor of a bucolic idyll to the Wilsons' course of life and to the chaste and innocent love of Fanny and Joseph (Joseph's song, we will remember, is that of a shepherd in an eclogue [II, 12]).[72]

"But no Blessings are pure in this World" (III, 3), observes Mr. Wilson with reference to the kidnapping of his son; and the cruel intrusion of the country squire upon this scene of contentment (III, 4) makes it clear that, for Fielding, there is no earthly paradise even away from London. "From the expulsion from Eden down to this day," he asserts in *Tom Jones* (XII, 12), no such Golden Age "ever had any existence, unless in the warm imaginations of the poets."[73] Barring uncontrollable accidents from without, Wilson's solution is nevertheless as close as possible to Fielding's ideal of the happy life, and it serves as a model for Joseph and Fanny to follow (IV, 16).

Mr. Wilson's long history, then, is not really a "digression" at all, but rather an integral part of the plan and purpose of *Joseph Andrews*. The broad allegory of the novel represents the pilgrimage of Joseph Andrews and Abraham Adams—like their Scriptural namesakes, Christian heroes exemplifying the essential virtues of the good man—from the vanity of the town to the relative naturalness and simplicity of the country. While the main narrative exposes selfishness and hypocrisy along the highway, Wilson's rake's progress through the vanities of London completes the panoramic satire of English society. His own career depicts the nearly fatal consequences of immorality and irreligion, the twin results of a faulty education. It is what might have happened to Joseph Andrews himself had he lacked the good advice and good example of Parson Adams. With Wilson's wise adoption of the classical ideal of life his own pilgrimage is complete, symbolically reinforcing the movement of the novel as a whole, and a moral alternative is established in contrast to the ways of vanity.

VII

Apology for the Clergy

A FURTHER important motive behind the good-humored didacticism of *Joseph Andrews* needs investigating, a motive that gives special point not only to the characterization of Adams as the true clergyman but also to the ridicule of the novel's corrupt and incompetent parsons. A persistent concern of Henry Fielding, Christian censor, was the "general neglect (I wish I could not say contempt) of religion."[1] Particularly disturbing to him was one manifestation of the impiety of the age—the prevalent contempt of the clergy. Unless the good reputation of the clergy could be preserved, he reasoned, the religion they represented would fall into contempt with them. Moral anarchy would result. From *The Champion* to *Amelia*, therefore, Fielding repeatedly spoke out in the effort to correct this "fashionable Vice of the Times,"[2] and to reform, within the Church, the individuals and conditions that occasioned it. These motives figure prominently in the moral purpose of *Joseph Andrews*.

Despite the good intentions of some historians who have tried to soften Macaulay's harsh description of the Restoration priesthood,[3] it is clear that the words "contempt of the clergy" were virtually "a stock phrase of the time."[4] Writers from the Restoration on regretted the low social position of the majority of those in orders, and many

Apology for the Clergy

tried to explain and rectify it, but disdain of the clergy was still very much in vogue when Fielding undertook the writing of *The Champion* and *Joseph Andrews*. In his *Angliae Notitia* (1669), Edward Chamberlayne thus lamented that the established clergy "are accounted by many, the Dross and Refuse of the nation."[5] The subject was also a frequent cause of complaint in South's sermons: "There is no nation or people under heaven, Christian or not Christian," he declared, "which despise, hate, and trample upon their clergy or priesthood comparably to the English."[6] Even Defoe, who spent much of his time attacking the Church, regretted that "the Office of a Minister . . . is but a Meanness in the Common Acceptation," and he saw the clergyman placed "on the Frontiers of Scandal . . . on a Stage of Reproach, to be palted [*sic*] by all the Agents of Atheism, and Prophaneness."[7] Swift, too, noticed that the priests of the Church of England went in "Fear of being choqued by Ribaldry, or Prophaneness," their gown "a general Mark of Contempt."[8] In *The Tatler*, No. 255 (November 25, 1710) and *The Guardian*, No. 163 (September 17, 1713), Steele similarly depicted the lowly position of the domestic chaplain. And just three years before Fielding began to write *Joseph Andrews*, Thomas Secker testified that "an open and professed Disregard to Religion" was "the distinguishing Character of the present Age":

Christianity is now ridiculed and railed at, with very little Reserve: and the Teachers of it, without any at all. Indeed with respect to us, the Rule which most of our Adversaries appear to have set themselves is, to be, at all adventures, as bitter as they can: and they follow it, not only beyond Truth, but beyond Probability: asserting the very worst things of us without foundation, and exaggerating every thing without mercy: imputing the Faults, and sometimes imaginary Faults, of particular Persons to the whole Order; and then declaiming against us all promiscuously, with such wild Vehemence, as in any Case but ours, they themselves would think, in the highest degree, unjust and cruel.[9]

More interesting as attempts to locate the causes of this widespread contempt of the priesthood are John Eachard's *The Grounds and Occasions of the Contempt of the Clergy and Religion* (1670), Lancelot Addison's *A Modest Plea for the Clergy* (1709), and John Hildrop's *The Contempt of the Clergy Considered,* published (significantly for our purposes) in 1739. Eachard's celebrated tract explained the trouble by reference "to two very plain things—the IGNORANCE of some, and the POVERTY of others of the Clergy."[10] Though at times leaning toward hyperbole, Eachard criticized the inadequate standards of education that pronounced a boy ready for the university if he could but scan a verse or recite his catechism; he resented the pedantry and the empty, affected oratory of some preachers; and he declared that many of those in orders were incapable of advising their parishioners in spiritual matters. Chiefly, however, it was the extreme poverty, the "mean condition," of the majority of the clergy that caused "their Sacred Profession [to be] much disparaged, and their Doctrine undervalued."[11] For the most part, livings were scarce and poor, and competed for by more clergymen than the country could accommodate. "I am confident," Eachard complained, "that, in a very little time, I could procure hundreds that should ride both sun and moon down, and be everlastingly yours! if you could help them but to a Living of £25 or £30 a year."[12]

Apology for the Clergy

Inevitably, the result of such conditions was the degradation of the priesthood. Consider, for example, Eachard's melancholy portrait of the fortunes of country chaplains:

Shall we trust them in some good Gentleman's house, there to perform holy things? With all my heart! so that they may not be called down from their studies to say Grace to every Health; that they may have a little better wages than the Cook or Butler; as also that there be a Groom in the house, besides the Chaplain (for sometimes to the £10 a year, they crowd [in] the looking after [a] couple of geldings): and that he may not be sent from table, picking his teeth, and sighing with his hat under his arm; whilst the Knight and my Lady eat up the tarts and chickens!

It may also be convenient, if he were suffered to speak now and then in the Parlour, besides at Grace and Prayer time; and that my cousin ABIGAIL and he sit not too near one another at meals, nor be presented together to the little vicarage! [13]

The parson was viewed by many of the gentry as another servant and a proper match for the lady's waiting woman. The plight of his offspring was, if anything, worse: "But to see Clergymen's children condemned to the walking [*holding*] of horses! to wait upon a tapster! or the like; and that only because their father was not able to allow them a more genteel education: these are such employments that cannot but bring great disgrace and dishonour upon the Clergy."[14]

Though Dean Lancelot Addison could not match his son Joseph's manner or wit, his *Modest Plea for the Clergy* is interesting as a rather partisan attempt to separate the real from the imaginary causes of "that *Obloquy* and *Contempt* which is heapt upon [the clergy]."[15] According to Addison, the most common complaints against the order—"want of Example," "Idleness," "Pride," and "Covetousness" — are "meer pretences, arising chiefly from Prejudice and *Mistake*."[16] These, he finds, are reasons invented by those who resent the diligent efforts of the priesthood to lead them from the paths of sin, or who falsely deem the true humility and poverty of the clergy worthy of contempt. But even this conscientious apologist will not shift all of the blame. He deplores the "eager hunting after Preferments, and Promotions" and "the scandalous abuses crept into the *Indulgence* of Pluralities" that were turning the Church into a market place.[17]

In 1739 this dismal situation, mainly a product of the evils of pluralism, absenteeism, and preferment-seeking, was no less severe. John Hildrop's summary of the charges leveled against the higher and lower clergy is convenient. Against the "Superior":

   I. Ambition and Avarice.
   II. Their servile Application and Attachment to Men in Power.
   III. The corrupt Use they make of their Revenues, their misapplying the Patrimony of the Church, which was designed for the Support of Charity and Hospitality, to Luxury and Vanity; and filling the most valuable Preferments with their own Children, Relations, and Sycophants, without any Respect so much as to a *Caeteris Paribus*.
   IV. Their Non-Residence, Pluralities, and Commendams.
   Those against the Inferior [are] general, indefinite, random Accusations, such as Pride, Pedantry, Ill-manners, Hypocrisy, Neglect of their Cures, and a long—long—&c.[18]

As we may remember from Parson Adams' argument with Barnabas (I, 17), these corrupt practices, which Hildrop

Apology for the Clergy

contradicts with more zeal than justification, were a favorite target for the reforming ardor of George Whitefield, who vehemently denounced "the indolent, earthly-minded, pleasure-taking clergy of the church of *England*," and stressed the need to "restore the church to its primitive dignity."[19]

More eloquent than either Hildrop or Whitefield, however, is Thomas Stackhouse's *The Miseries and Great Hardships of the Inferior Clergy; and a Modest Plea for their Rights and better Usage* (1722), a work valuable for its full and lively representation of the state of the Church and the clergy in the early part of the century. While favored members of the Church proudly flourished "at *Tunbridge* or *Bath,* and at the *Court of Requests*"[20] on the emoluments of plural livings, their curates, saddled with the care of the parish, languished in disrespect on stipends averaging thirty pounds a year.[21] Such is the state of affairs depicted by Stackhouse. He bitterly reproves the negligent and worldly among the higher clergy, "those that see not their Parishes above once in a Quarter, and perhaps that too with a View to the Profits more than the Souls of them."[22] Many are proud and contemptuous of their subordinates—"mighty Rectors riding over the Heads of their Readers and Curates";[23] others are ambitious time-servers, "hunting about for more Preferments, and making what they have *Livings and Emoluments* in the most carnal Sense of the Words."[24]

In contrast, consider, with Parson Adams in mind, the condition of the poor curate:

Oh my Lord, how prettily and temperately may a Wife and half a dozen Children be maintain'd with almost thirty Pounds *per Annum*? What an handsom Shift will an ingenious and frugal Divine make to take it by turns, and wear a Cassock one Year, and a Pair of Breeches another? What a primitive Sight will it be, to see a Man of God with his Shoes out at Toes, and his Stockings out at Heels, wandering about in an old Russet Coat, or a tatter'd Gown, for Apprentices to point at, and Wags to break Jests on? And what a notable Figure will he make in a Pulpit on Sundays, that has sent his *Hooker* and *Stillingfleet,* his *Pearson* and *Sanderson,* his *Barrow* and *Tillotson,* with many more Fathers of the *English* Church, into Limbo long since, to keep his Wife's pensive Petticoat Company, and her much lamented Wedding-Ring?[25]

The inferior clergy were ignorant for want of books, despised for the meanness of their dress. Forbidden upon pain of excommunication to "follow any Trade or worldly Labour," and with no one willing to publish their sermons,[26] curates found it nearly impossible honorably to supplement their meager stipends. Some, like Parson Adams, earned a few extra shillings by teaching school or serving several curacies.[27] Others preferred to truckle to the rich, "the sordid Humour of creeping and cringing to wealthy Tables."[28] The rest, it would seem, could starve with a good conscience. In all, then, the lot of the inferior clergy was "Contempt and Penury, in a despised Calling."[29]

The objective of much of Fielding's writing, in both the novels and the journals, was to remove this contempt and its causes. "Not only the Man of Piety," he declared in *The Jacobite's Journal,* No. 32 (July 9, 1748), "but even he who professes a decent Regard to Religion, as to a wholesome, civil Institution, must agree in the Necessity of preserving the Priesthood from the Contempt of the People." One way to preserve the clergy from contempt was, of course, the exposure and elimination of its rotten

Apology for the Clergy

members—the Murdertexts, Puzzletexts, and Tickletexts who parade through Fielding's works, twisting Scripture and religion to their own advantage; hypocritical priests whose only sense of "calling" is, as Jack Commons says in *The Letter Writers*, "the promise of a good living."[30]

Indeed, the catalogue of clerical vices that Fielding tirelessly assaulted is formidable—among others, luxury, pluralism, selfishness, pride, bigotry, sycophancy, and ignorance. He was suspicious of those who "desire to maintain the honour of the cloth by living like gentlemen, which would, perhaps, be better maintained by living unlike them."[31] Like Allworthy, he sensed the equivocation of Thwackum and his kind, who wrote to the good squire: "Your objection to pluralities is being righteous over-much. If there were any crime in the practice, so many godly men would not agree to it."[32] We may recall, too, the pluralist parson of *A Journey from this World to the Next* (I, 7), who, for lack of charity, is locked out of Elysium; or the proud young cleric in *Amelia* (IX, 8), who disputes with Dr. Harrison the plain meaning of a scriptural injunction to charity. Particularly objectionable to Fielding was the intolerant orthodoxy of the ordinary in *Jonathan Wild* (IV, 1), like Thwackum refusing to admit the salvation of any who lie outside the pale of the Church. And the weakness of many of the clergy is satirized in the obsequious, pedantic Parson Supple — "a good-natured, worthy man," but, "to please his palate" at Squire Western's table, rather too willing to shirk the duties of his office.[33]

Such portraits as those above—only a few of the many to be found in his works—reveal Fielding's continuing efforts to expose the corruption and incompetence that were partially responsible for the contempt of the clergy. For the prevalence of this attitude, "the government is to blame," says the clergyman in *Amelia* (IX, 10), his pride smarting from the insults of several young bucks in Vauxhall Gardens. "Are not books of infidelity, treating our holy religion as a mere imposture, nay, sometimes as a mere jest, published daily, and spread abroad amongst the people with perfect impunity?" With this Dr. Harrison agrees, but places a share of the responsibility on the shoulders of the clergy themselves, many of whom, by the bad example of their own lives, justify the disrespect they are shown:

". . . the whole blame doth not lie [with the government]; some little share of the fault is, I am afraid, to be imputed to the clergy themselves. . . . They are not taxed with giving any other support to infidelity than what it draws from the ill examples of their lives; I mean of the lives of some of them. Here too the laity carry their censures too far; for there are very few or none of the clergy whose lives, if compared with those of the laity, can be called profligate; but such, indeed, is the perfect purity of our religion, such is the innocence and virtue which it exacts to entitle us to its glorious rewards and to screen us from its dreadful punishments, that he must be a very good man indeed who lives up to it. Thus then these persons argue. This man is educated in a perfect knowledge of religion, is learned in its laws, and is by his profession obliged, in a manner, to have them always before his eyes. The rewards which it promises to the obedience of these laws are so great, and the punishments threatened on disobedience so dreadful, that it is impossible but all men must fearfully fly from the one, and as eagerly pursue the other. If, therefore, such a person lives in direct opposition to, and in a constant breach of, these laws, the inference is obvious."[34]

Apology for the Clergy

True, some of the priesthood were corrupt, but this did not excuse the public inclination "to ascribe the Faults of particular Members of a Profession to the Profession itself, and thence to derive Ridicule and Contempt on the whole," a practice that contributed—and this is the real point—"to the no small Advancement of Irreligion and Immorality, by lessening that Awe and Respect which we ought to bear towards a Body of Men, who are particularly appointed to instruct us in the Ways of true Piety and Virtue, and who generally deserve the utmost Regard from us."[35] Many of the clergy were truly devout and conscientious—diligent in their office and exemplary in their lives. Even such men as Parson Adams, however, were commonly and unjustly ridiculed for another reason: their poverty. Poverty, Fielding observed, had perhaps "brought more Contempt on our own Clergy, than hath been cast upon them by the utmost Malice of Infidels or Libertines."[36] In the effort to remedy this injustice, he alluded in the novels to the distresses of the clergy and their families, and he took up the problem at length in *The Jacobite's Journal* (Nos. 21 and 29-32), where he warmly recommended the establishment of a public charity for the widows and children of the inferior clergy. In *Tom Jones,* for example, he more dramatically resumed the pleas of the *Journal* by making both Mrs. Honour and Goody Seagrim the descendants of indigent parsons. Lest his point be missed, he added a note:

> This [Mrs. Honour] is the second person of low condition whom we have recorded in this history to have sprung from the clergy. It is to be hoped such instances will, in future ages, when some provision is made for the families of the inferior clergy, appear stranger than they can be thought at present.[37]

Again, in *Amelia*, Mrs. Bennet is the daughter of a worthy, but poor, clergyman whose salary was less than £40 a year. Mrs. Ellison says of her: "She was the daughter of a clergyman, had little or no fortune, and married a poor parson for love, who left her in the utmost distress."[38] Unless the clergyman could provide a comfortable living for himself and family, Fielding feared, he would bring "a Contempt on his sacred Function" and lose "all that Respect which every Man must preserve, who, with due Efficacy, will discharge the sacerdotal Duties."[39]

The earliest and most extensive document in Fielding's program to check the public contempt of the priesthood is the "Apology for the Clergy," a series of four essays published in *The Champion* in the spring of 1740 (March 29 and April 5, 12, and 19). These articles are extremely important to a right reading of *Joseph Andrews*, for they furnish in theory what the novel dramatizes at length: that is, with a design to explain and correct the contempt of the clergy, they delineate the characters of the true and false clergyman. We have already seen that the "Apology" provides a kind of preliminary study of the good Parson Adams, who pre-eminently exhibits the three basic characteristics of the true priest—humility, charity, and poverty. "Can such a man as this," asks Fielding, "be the object of contempt? or can any be more entitled to respect and honour?" Anticipating Adams' encounter with the "roasting" squire and his confederates (III, 7), he answers that only "boys and beaus, and madmen, and rakes, and fools, and villains, may laugh at this sacred person; may shake those ridiculous heads at him which would have been flung in the face of a Socrates or a Plato."[40] The only just source of reproach is the bad character of some

Apology for the Clergy

of the clergy. Fielding's portrait of the false minister is lengthy, but it may be reproduced as a kind of composite sketch of the Trullibers, Thwackums, and Supples:

> Let us suppose then, a man of loose morals, proud, malevolent, vain, rapacious, and revengeful; not grieving at, but triumphing over the sins of men, and rejoicing, like the devil, that they will be punished for them; deaf to the cries of the poor; shunning the distressed; blind to merit; a magnifier and spreader of slander; not shunning the society of the wicked for fear of contamination, but from hypocrisy and vain glory; hating not vice but the vicious; resenting not only an injury, but the least affront with inveteracy. Let us suppose this man feasting himself luxuriously at the tables of the great, where he is suffered at the expense of flattering their vices, and often too, as meanly submitting to see himself and his order, nay often religion itself, ridiculed, whilst, that he may join in the Burgundy, he joins in the laugh, or rather is laughed at by the fools he flatters. Suppose him going hence (perhaps in his chariot), through the streets, and contemptuously overlooking a man of merit and learning in distress. *Proh Deum atque hominum fidem!* Is this a Christian?—Perhaps it will be said I have drawn a monster, and not a portrait taken from life. God forbid it should; but it is not sufficient that the whole does not resemble; for he who hath but an eye, a nose, a single feature in this deformed figure, can challenge none of the honours due to a minister of the Gospel.[41]

Fielding insists that, though the order as a whole must not be charged with the malpractices of some of its individuals, neither must the order shield its members from just censure: "For as nothing can hurt religion so much as a contempt of the clergy, so nothing can justify, or indeed cause any such contempt but their own bad lives."[42]

A Study of *Joseph Andrews*

Fielding's apology for the clergy was continued, in fictional form, as an important theme in *Joseph Andrews*. But Parson Adams, designed as an image of the faithful clergyman, was misunderstood by some at least of his readers (then as now). Among these were Fielding's political enemies, such as Porcupinus Pelagius, who accused him of having "ridiculed all the inferior Clergy in the dry, unnatural Character of Parson *Adams*."[43] And a contributor to *The Student* had to defend the parson against the objections of sophisticated clergymen.[44] We may in a way be grateful for such criticism, however, since it prompted Sarah Fielding to interject into *The Cry* an important explanation of her brother's motives in creating Adams. After asserting that the hero of the true comic epic (Don Quixote, for example) is both virtuous and sympathetic, she remarks:

Nor less [mis]understood [than Don Quixote] is the character of parson *Adams* in *Joseph Andrews* by those persons, who, fixing their thoughts on the hounds trailing the bacon in his pocket (with some oddnesses in his behaviour, and peculiarities in his dress) think proper to overlook the noble simplicity of his mind, with the other innumerable beauties in his character; which, to those who can understand *the word to the wise*, are placed in the most conspicuous view.

That the ridiculers of parson *Adams* are designed to be the proper objects of ridicule (and not that innocent man himself) is a truth which the author hath in many places set in the most glaring light. And lest his meaning should be perversely misunderstood, he hath fully displayed his own sentiments on that head, by writing a whole scene, in which such laughers are properly treated, and their characters truly depicted.[45]

Apology for the Clergy

In a note she identifies the scene as Book III, chapter 7, which Fielding pointedly entitled, "A scene of roasting, very nicely adapted to the present taste and times." "The characters," Sarah observes, "are an old half-pay officer, a dull poet, a scraping fiddler, and a lame *German* dancing-master." Unless Fielding himself had told us, we could scarcely have more authoritative testimony that an important purpose of *Joseph Andrews* was the correction of one harmful aspect of "the present taste and times"—that is, the contempt of the clergy.

The Preface to *Joseph Andrews* gives a reason for the prominence of this theme in the novel. Adams is a clergyman, Fielding explains, because "no other office could have given him so many Opportunities of displaying his worthy Inclinations"; no other office, in other words, could be so effective an instrument for social good. At the same time, Fielding, with one significant qualification, declares his affection for the gentlemen of Adams' cloth, "for whom, while they are worthy of their sacred Order, no Man can possibly have a greater respect." Beside Adams and serving as foils to him, there are no fewer than six clergymen in *Joseph Andrews,* of whom Barnabas and Trulliber are most memorable; all six are corrupt or incompetent, unworthy of their order.

Barnabas and Trulliber are lively dramatizations of the negligent, worldly, and hypocritical parsons who were subverting the function and dignity of the Church. We will remember Barnabas (I, 13-17)—ignorant, pleasure-loving custodian of the punch bowl; perfunctory and incapable in his offices to Joseph; vain of his sermons and his knowledge of the law; willing to extoll the virtues of a reprobate if the price were right. He vigorously denounces the only doctrine of Whitefield's preaching worth preserving (in the opinion of Adams and Fielding):

> "Whoever prints such Heterodox Stuff ought to be hanged," says Barnabas. "Sir," said he, turning to Adams, "this Fellow's Writings (I know not whether you have seen them) are levelled at the Clergy. He would reduce us to the Example of the Primitive Ages, forsooth! and would insinuate to the People that a Clergyman ought to be always preaching and praying. He pretends to understand the Scripture literally; and would make Mankind believe that the Poverty and low Estate which was recommended to the Church in its Infancy, and was only temporary Doctrine adapted to her under Persecution, was to be preserved in her flourishing and established State. Sir, the Principles of Toland, Woolston, and all the Free Thinkers, are not calculated to do half the Mischief, as those professed by this Fellow and his Followers." (I, 17)

But Trulliber is worse (II, 14-15) — avaricious, proud, hypocritical; a man better suited to tending his hogs than to caring for the souls of his parishioners. He is, indeed, "a Parson on Sundays, but all the other six might more properly be called a Farmer" (II, 14), a practice that makes him a violator of Church law.[46] Despite his professions of faith, Trulliber's knowledge of the Scriptures does not extend to the injunctions to charity. And his great authority in his parish is founded upon his own wealth and hypocrisy, and the fear that he inspires in his parishioners: "Mr. Trulliber had by his Professions of Piety, by his Gravity, Austerity, Reserve, and the Opinion of his great Wealth, so great an Authority in his Parish, that they all lived in the utmost Fear and Apprehension of him" (II, 15). With Adams, we may believe, Fielding "was sorry to see such Men in Orders" (II, 14).

Apology for the Clergy

The other clergymen in the novel appear briefly or are merely mentioned. There is the ignorant parson—newly created for the revised second edition of the novel[47]—who, "putting on his Spectacles and Gravity together," knowingly pronounced Adams' Aeschylus "a Manuscript of one of the Fathers": "Ay, aye, Question and Answer [.] The Beginning is the Catechism in Greek" (II, 11). And there is the politically minded rector who formerly expelled Adams from his curacy for not influencing an election against his conscience (II, 8). Worse than these, however, is the spiteful parson of Adams' parish, a man who takes pleasure in the ruin of his parishioners:

> The Parson had for many Years lived in a constant State of Civil War, or, which is perhaps as bad, of Civil Law, with Sir Thomas himself and the Tenants of his Manor. The Foundation of this Quarrel was a Modus, by setting which aside, an Advantage of several shillings *per annum* would have accrued to the Rector; but he had not yet been able to accomplish his Purpose, and had reaped hitherto nothing better from the Suits than the pleasure (which he used indeed frequently to say was no small one) of reflecting that he had utterly undone many of the poor Tenants, though he had at the same time greatly impoverished himself. (I, 3)

Finally we may recall the haughty priest who invites contempt by his utter lack of that humility which, Fielding had insisted, was essential to the true clergyman. The false promiser thus applauds Adams' fatherly love of his flock, but laments that such sentiments are not universal among the clergy:

> "I am sorry to say the Parson of our Parish, instead of esteeming his Poor Parishioners as a part of his Family, seems rather

to consider them as not of the same Species with himself. He seldom speaks to any, unless some few of the richest of us; nay, indeed, he will not move his Hat to the others. I often laugh when I behold him on Sundays strutting along the Church-Yard like a Turky-Cock through Rows of his Parishioners, who bow to him with as much Submission, and are as unregarded, as a sett of servile Courtiers by the proudest Prince in Christendom. But if such temporal Pride is ridiculous, surely the spiritual is odious and detestable; if such a puffed-up empty human Bladder, strutting in princely Robes, justly moves one's Derision, surely in the Habit of a Priest it must raise our Scorn." (II, 16)

In such portraits as these Fielding halted his narrative to lash at the ignorance, ambition, malice, vainglory, and worldliness of some of the clergy, to expose those corruptions that were rendering the priesthood ineffective and contemptible.

In his reply to the promising gentleman, however, Adams upholds the character of the clergy in general and, with a rare touch of bitterness, speaks out against "the Readiness which too many of the Laity show to contemn the Order." These sentiments, as we have seen, underlie Fielding's apology. While the hyprocrite Trulliber is held in awe, the good Adams, though loved and respected by those that know him, suffers ridicule because of his poverty. Like Stackhouse, Fielding regrets that penury and contempt are the lot of too many honest clergymen, and in the character of Parson Adams he dramatizes the injustice of this situation. With his "handsome Income of twenty-three Pounds a-Year," Fielding observes, Adams "could not make any great Figure . . . because he lived in a dear country, and was a little incumbered with a

Apology for the Clergy

Wife and six Children" (I, 3). We remember him, with his cassock torn "about ten Years ago in passing over a Stile" (II, 14), taking a cup of ale in the squire's kitchen (I, 2). With no other way of augmenting his salary—no one will publish his sermons (I, 17)—and with small hope of advancement under the misused patronage system,[48] Adams must earn a few extra shillings by teaching and by preaching regularly at four churches (II, 8). His family similarly suffers: because he cannot afford a university education for him, his son—despite "an infinite Stock of Learning" and "an unexceptionable Life"—is refused ordination (II, 8); and his eldest daughter must hope only to succeed Mrs. Slipslop (IV, 8), herself the daughter of a clergyman (I, 3). Under these circumstances, it is not surprising that the proud Sir Thomas and his lady should regard Adams disdainfully "as a kind of Domestic only, belonging to the Parson of the Parish" (I, 3).

At the end of the novel, *deus ex machina,* Adams and his family are rescued from their poverty when Mr. Booby persuades the reluctant parson to accept his offer of a second living of £130 a year: "He at first refused it, resolving not to quit his Parishioners, with whom he had lived so long; but, on recollecting he might keep a Curate at this Living, he hath been lately inducted into it" (IV, 16). As we have seen, no one has less patience than Fielding with the abuses of pluralism and nonresidence, but, he ironically implies, while the revenue of the Church remained in the pockets of a few bishops, plural livings were the only way by which a poor clergyman could keep from starving.

As Sarah Fielding pointed out, Book III, chapter 7, is the key to the apology for the clergy in *Joseph Andrews.*

A Study of *Joseph Andrews*

"Very nicely adapted to the present taste and times," the "roasting" of Adams by the squire and his parasites is, in fact, a vivid dramatization of that unjustified contempt of the clergy that was undermining the cause of religion. After enduring the series of jests and pranks practiced upon him, Adams' patience at last gives out, and he speaks rather eloquently in reproof of his tormentors:

"Sir, I am sorry to see one to whom Providence hath been so bountiful in bestowing his Favours make so ill and ungrateful a Return for them; for, though you have not insulted me yourself, it is visible you have delighted in those that do it, nor have once discouraged the many Rudenesses which have been shown towards me; indeed, towards yourself, if you rightly understood them; for I am your Guest, and by the Laws of Hospitality entitled to your Protection. One Gentleman hath thought proper to produce some Poetry upon me, of which I shall only say, that I had rather be the Subject than the Composer. He hath pleased to treat me with Disrespect as a Parson. I apprehend my Order is not the subject of scorn, nor that I can become so, unless by being a Disgrace to it, which I hope Poverty will never be called. Another Gentleman, indeed, hath repeated some Sentences, where the Order itself is mentioned with Contempt. He says they are taken from Plays. I am sure such Plays are a Scandal to the Government which permits them, and cursed will be the Nation where they are represented. How others have treated me I need not observe; they themselves, when they reflect, must allow the Behaviour to be as improper to my Years as to my Cloth." (III, 7)

This passage is the culmination of an important theme in *Joseph Andrews*. With Adams, Fielding believed that the priesthood itself was not "the subject of scorn" unless

Apology for the Clergy

rendered so by the disgraceful conduct of its members. He recognized that the poverty of the clergy, far from being a disgrace, was rather a sign of their being true followers of Christ. Still, poverty should not mean a life of destitution and contempt; and, as we have seen, he worked to alleviate the miseries and hardships of the inferior clergy. For the good of society, Fielding felt, the characters of men like Parson Adams must be protected, and the religion they represented must be preserved from ridicule.

VIII

Conclusion

BY HIS OWN admission, metaphysics and gravity were not congenial to Fielding. As a thinker, he would rather be right than profound, sensible than systematic. In *The Champion* (January 5, 1739/40), for example, he made this only partly ironic confession:

> Among the sciences (of all which, I thank heaven, I am entirely ignorant) I have been always the greatest enemy to the metaphysics. A science I cannot help imagining to have been invented with a design rather to puzzle and darken truth, than to explain and enlighten it.
>
> There is no word in the English language, for which I have so great a contempt as for the word reasoning.[1]

He liked to scoff at those captious theorists, like his own philosopher Square, whose chop-logic speculations were inadequate to the business of life. And as a moralist he preferred the laughing mode of satire to Richardson's sober style. He chose, as he variously put it, to speak truth with a smiling countenance, to laugh mankind out of their favorite follies and vices, to tickle them into good manners.

Yet behind the satirist's mask, beneath all the hearty common sense of comedy, there were two things at least that he thought about long and seriously: they were, to use his own analogy in *Amelia* (I, 1), the complex arts

Conclusion

of fiction and life. The two, he felt, were intimately related. By the practice of his craft, the novelist aimed not only to delight his reader but to instruct him in the shaping of that greater artifact, the good man. These motives underlie *Joseph Andrews*.

There were, to be sure, other and more practical reasons for writing the novel. For one thing, Fielding desperately needed the money. After the Licensing Act of 1737 had shut the doors of the theatre against him, he had tried to earn a living as a lawyer, political journalist, and occasional hackney writer, but none of these resources proved adequate to support him and his family. Late in 1741 he found himself in debt and neglected by his friends among the Patriots, his wife ill and his favorite daughter dying. In an effort to brighten the gloom of the winter, he turned to fiction and labored, with incredible detachment, to write the first masterful comic novel in English.

A satire of the immensely popular *Pamela*, he must have thought, was sure to be financially profitable. But what is more, Richardson's pretentious book—as the noise of applause, even from those who should have known better, convinced him—needed to be castigated and corrected. It was bad morality and bad art. In *Shamela*, his brilliant parody, Fielding had ridiculed the absurdities of Richardson's novel; in *Joseph Andrews* he began a rival tradition.

This new species of writing, as he called it, was the product as well of a considered and, for its time, remarkably sophisticated theory of the art of the novel. In the effort to lend dignity to the contemned genre of prose fiction, Fielding claimed to have written not a mere romance, but an epic, in this case "a comic Epic Poem in Prose," whose aim was the exposure of "the true Ridicu-

A Study of *Joseph Andrews*

lous" in society—affectation and its twin sources, vanity and hypocrisy. In the Preface the satirist implicitly acknowledged his responsibility as censor of the manners, taste, and morality of his age. "The satirist," he had said in *The Champion* (March 27, 1740), "is to be regarded as our physician, not our enemy."[2] In *Joseph Andrews* the selfishness of the lawyer, the avarice of Peter Pounce, the hypocrisy of Parson Trulliber, the lust of Lady Booby, the bad art of *Pamela*—all are laid bare by the knife of ridicule. Fielding's laughter is purposeful.

And his purpose is Christian. The theory of good nature and the message of good works that inform the novels and their heroes comprise an ethic of social amelioration. It is a Pelagian ethic formulated in countless latitudinarian sermons, but most notably for our purposes in those of Barrow, Tillotson, Clarke, and Hoadly. These liberal divines, whose work Fielding read and admired, preached the essential perfectibility of man, if only assisted by good education and good example to the proper exercise of his reason and will. Even the virtuous and charitable infidel, they asserted, might earn his salvation. As Fielding was writing *Joseph Andrews*, however, this pragmatic, common-sense Christianity was being challenged by the Antinomianism and reforming zeal of George Whitefield. The antagonism between the Establishment and the Methodists brought the issue of faith versus works into sharp relief, reviving, in effect, the old quarrel between St. Augustine and Pelagius. The dispute served to focus the doctrine of benevolence in *Joseph Andrews*. Most explicit in Adams' denunciation of Whitefield and Trulliber, a recurring theme of the novel is that, without good works, faith and knowledge and ritual are dead; that charity,

Conclusion

not "Nonsense and Enthusiasm," works for the health of society and of the private soul.

With Whitefield, however, Fielding did find one thing in common: the desire to return the priesthood to the ideals of primitive Christianity. By so doing, he felt, the clergy would remove from themselves the taint of pride and luxury, the only valid cause of that prevalent contempt of their order that was impairing their usefulness to society. In the good Parson Adams and in the incompetent and pharisaical priests of *Joseph Andrews,* we find the fictional dramatization of types adumbrated earlier in the "Apology for the Clergy," wherein Fielding had affirmed the dignity of the priesthood while decrying the corruption of some of its members. The true clergyman was the indispensable custodian of the public morality.

A writer with firm Christian convictions seriously exploring the potentialities of the epic form for the first time in an English novel, Fielding discovered within both traditions—the homiletic and the literary—useful suggestions for the meaning and method of *Joseph Andrews.* This raw material, shaped into art, gave purpose and unity to the rambling peregrinations of his heroes and made of his novel something much more than the conventional picaresque tale. As the moral antithesis to vanity and self-seeking, he proposed the practical ethos of the latitudinarians and the Christian heroism of the good man, whose comprehensive virtues of charity and chastity, as Tillotson and Hoadly had said, summed up religion. Taking another hint from Isaac Barrow and the divines, Fielding linked in a contemporary setting the humorous fortunes of the good man's biblical prototypes, Abraham and Joseph—now, in a less heroic age, a quixotic parson and a

A Study of *Joseph Andrews*

virtuous footman—and set his pilgrims wayfaring in a land at once familiar and alien, their pilgrimage symbolically prefigured in Mr. Wilson's progress from the vanity of the town to a simple country life of wisdom and love according to the classical ideal. As they act out their spiritual odyssey of the road, we are amused at the innocence of these good men, but we laugh with contempt at those beaus and coquettes, parsons and pettifoggers, innkeepers and squires whose cupidity that innocence helps to expose.

Among students of Fielding and the novel, *Joseph Andrews* has survived as a kind of lovable curiosity, valued less for itself than for what it led to—*Tom Jones* and the tradition of Dickens and Thackeray. Everyone, of course, has admired its hearty comic scenes and robust humanity. But, as a work of art and morality, it has been treated with condescension. We have not, I think, understood what Fielding intended and what he achieved. For all its uproarious good humor, *Joseph Andrews* is ultimately a moral book. For all its apparent artlessness, it is the work of a conscious craftsman.

Notes

ABBREVIATIONS

Editions

Baker ed.: Sheridan W. Baker, Jr., ed., *An Apology for the Life of Mrs. Shamela Andrews, By Henry Fielding*, Berkeley and Los Angeles, 1953.

Henley ed.: William Ernest Henley, ed., *The Complete Works of Henry Fielding, Esq.*, 16 vols., London, 1903.

Jensen ed.: Gerard Edward Jensen, ed., *The Covent-Garden Journal, By Sir Alexander Drawcansir, Knt. Censor of Great Britain (Henry Fielding)*, 2 vols., New Haven, 1915.

Periodicals

ELH: *[Journal of English Literary History]*
JHI: *Journal of the History of Ideas*
MLN: *Modern Language Notes*
N&Q: *Notes and Queries*
PQ: *Philological Quarterly*
RES: *Review of English Studies*
SP: *Studies in Philology*

A Study of *Joseph Andrews*

Preface

1. Throughout this book, quotations from *Joseph Andrews* are taken from J. Paul de Castro, ed., *The Adventures of Joseph Andrews*, London, 1929. Roman and arabic numerals indicate, respectively, the book and chapter of the novel wherein the quotation or reference will be found.

2. "In Defense of Fielding," in *Unprofessional Essays* (London, 1956), p. 49.

3. "The Background of Fielding's Laughter," *ELH*, in press.

I: Introduction

1. Alan Dugald McKillop, *Samuel Richardson: Printer and Novelist* (Chapel Hill, 1936), p. 43. McKillop's excellent study thoroughly discusses the progress of *Pamela*'s popularity (pp. 42-106).

2. Anna Laetitia Barbauld, ed., *The Correspondence of Samuel Richardson* (London, 1804), IV, 286; *Shamela*, Baker ed., p. 13.

3. *The Gentleman's Magazine*, XI (January, 1741), 56.

4. *The Works of the Late Aaron Hill, Esq.*, 2nd ed. (London, 1754), II, 130.

5. Fielding seems to have felt that the clergy, by their unprecedented public applause of *Pamela*—a mere romance, and to him a silly and immoral one—were giving further cause to the regrettable contempt of their order that was then prevalent. In *Shamela* the foolish Parson Tickletext is shown to be among the London clergy who "have made it [their] common Business here, not only to cry it up, but to preach it up likewise: The Pulpit, as well as the Coffee-house, hath resounded with its Praise, and it is expected shortly, that his L——p will recommend it in a [pastoral] Letter to our whole Body." (Baker ed., p. 9.)

6. In a letter to Richardson from Bath in February, James Leake quotes Pope as saying that *Pamela* "will do more good than many volumes of sermons." (*Correspondence,* Barbauld ed., I, lix.) The poet's estimate of the novel seems to have spread quickly through London. In *Shamela*'s parody of the "puffs" that Richardson prefixed to the second edition of *Pamela,* Fielding burlesqued Pope's remark:

Notes

"[*Pamela*] will do more good than the C[*lerg*]y have done harm in the World." (Baker ed., p. 7.)

7. *The Champion* (May 17, 1740).

8. Leo Hughes, "The Influence of Fielding's Milieu upon His Humor," *University of Texas Studies in English, 1944* (Austin, 1945), p. 287. Those who share this view are legion. Some scholars, of course, have doubted the parody hypothesis: see, for example, Aurélien Digeon, *Les Romans de Fielding* (Paris, 1923), p. 78; Arnold Kettle, *An Introduction to the English Novel* (London, 1951), I, 73; and Charles B. Woods, "Fielding and the Authorship of *Shamela*," *PQ*, XXV (1946), 271. Of these, Professor Woods is most cogent; he wisely stresses the important distinction between parodic imitation and satiric contrast.

9. Other examples of parody, of course, occasionally occur— e.g., the imitations of Richardson's epistolary method (I, 6, 10) and, with a less specific target, the panegyric to Love "in the sublime style" (I, 7).

10. "Criticism and Parody," *Thought*, XXVI (1951), 185. But Davis, like most of Fielding's critics, nevertheless assumes that *Joseph Andrews* began as a parody (p. 190). In fact, those scholars whose study of the burlesque mode ought to have made them most suspicious of this fallacy have been, strangely enough, among its chief perpetuators. See, for example, Archibald B. Shepperson, *The Novel in Motley: A History of the Burlesque Novel in English* (Cambridge, Mass., 1936), p. 30, and George Kitchin, *A Survey of Burlesque and Parody in English* (Edinburgh, 1931), p. 167.

11. The critics who maintain that Adams, as we remember him, was largely conceived after Book I, chapter 14 (his arrival at the Dragon Inn), overlook his introduction in chapter 3, where he is presented with all of his winning characteristics. His erudition, benevolence, affability, courtesy, courage, piety, poverty, and especially his quixotic simplicity—all are deliberately established. He is furthermore kept in mind by passages in chapters 6, 10, and 11. The Preface, of course, with its apology for Adams, was probably written after the novel itself.

12. Among those who hold to this position, wholly or in part, are Digeon, pp. 67-69; J. Paul de Castro, ed., *Joseph Andrews*, pp. 10-11; H. K. Banerji, *Henry Fielding: Playwright, Journalist and Master of the Art of Fiction* (Oxford, 1929), p. 109; Brian W. Downs, ed., *An Apology for the Life of Mrs. Shamela Andrews* (Cambridge,

1930), pp. ix-x; and F. Homes Dudden, *Henry Fielding: His Life, Works, and Times* (Oxford, 1952), I, 325.

13. *The London Magazine*, X (June, 1741), 304.

14. In *The Age of Johnson, Essays Presented to Chauncey Brewster Tinker* (New Haven, 1949), pp. 139-148. Others, however, more or less anticipated Work's position. Fielding's relation to the Low Church party was pointed out, for example, in Mary Elizabeth Branch's unpublished thesis, "Fielding's Attitude Toward the Chief Religious Groups of His Time" (Chicago, 1926); and Charles B. Woods' judicious article on the authorship of *Shamela* placed Fielding staunchly on the side of the clerical opponents of Whitefield (*PQ*, XXV [1946], 262-268). For defining the Christian content of *The Champion* and proposing its general pertinence to Fielding's subsequent writings, however, Professor Work deserves most of the credit for inaugurating the current re-evaluation.

15. *Tom Jones*, V, 2; Henley ed., III, 212.

16. *Die Philosophie Fieldings,* Kölner Anglistische Arbeiten, Bd. XV (Leipzig, 1932), 11.

17. Digeon, pp. 260-262.

18. *Of the Remedy of Affliction for the Loss of Our Friends,* Henley ed., XVI, 109. Previously, in the same essay, Fielding remarked that the rigid, unfeeling Stoicism of a Stilpo "hath no charms for me" (p. 99). For further discussion of Fielding's views on Stoicism, see below, pp. 66-68.

19. *The Works of Samuel Johnson, LL.D., Together with His life, and Notes on His Lives of the Poets* (London, 1787), I, 215.

20. *The History of Henry Fielding* (New Haven, 1918), II, 212.

21. "Fielding and Empirical Realism," in *Philosophical Parallelisms in Six English Novelists: The Conception of Good, Evil and Human Nature* (Philadelphia, 1929), p. 46.

22. *The Champion* for November 20, 1739, quotes from "the excellent Lord Shaftesbury, in his Advice to an Author." (*The Champion: Containing a Series of Papers, Humorous, Moral, Political and Critical,* 2nd ed. [London, 1743], I, 13.) And in the Preface to *Joseph Andrews* Fielding partially concurs with the low opinion of mere burlesque expressed in *An Essay on the Freedom of Wit and Humour.* Other references are in *The Champion,* March 11 and 13, 1739/40. See also below, pp. 62-64.

23. See "Suggestions Toward a Genealogy of the 'Man of Feeling,'" *ELH*, I (1934), 205-230.

Notes

II: The Christian Background

1. Toward the close of Fielding's career the influence of "our favourite Dr. Barrow" is obvious in *Amelia* (1751) and *The Covent-Garden Journal* (1752). In *Amelia* (XII, 5) the moral reconstruction of Captain Booth is occasioned by his perusal of Barrow's works while imprisoned in a sponging house. One of Barrow's sermons, "The Duty and Reward of Bounty to the Poor," is quoted in several places in *The Covent-Garden Journal*, namely in Nos. 29, 39, 44, and 69. No one has as yet noticed, however, that Barrow's influence upon Fielding was making itself felt, and significantly, as early as *Joseph Andrews*. For a number of reasons I believe that Fielding's familiarity with the writings of this important divine began about August, 1741, just before he started writing the novel: (1) I have uncovered no specific instance of Barrow's name or thought in Fielding's previous writing, whereas (2) his influence upon *Joseph Andrews*, as we shall find, seems clear; and (3) Fielding's only known copy of Barrow's *Works* was the edition issued in August of 1741. (See the catalogue of Fielding's library reprinted in the appendix to Ethel M. Thornbury, *Henry Fielding's Theory of the Comic Prose Epic*, University of Wisconsin Studies in Language and Literature, No. 30 [Madison, 1931], p. 183.) *The London Magazine*, X, 416, lists the 1741 edition as issued in August for Tonson and Andrew Millar, who was shortly to publish *Joseph Andrews*.

Fielding also frequently acknowledged his respect for Tillotson, Clarke, and Hoadly. Both the style and the substance of Archbishop Tillotson's sermons, for example, are recommended in *Joseph Andrews* (I, 16). Other allusions to him occur in *The Champion* for January 22, 1739/40, where he is linked with Samuel Clarke, and for March 15, 1739/40; and he is cited again, along with Barrow and Clarke, in *The Covent-Garden Journal*, No. 4. In addition to the two references just mentioned, Clarke's influence upon *Amelia* (I, 3) has been indicated by A. R. Towers, "Fielding and Dr. Samuel Clarke," *MLN*, LXX (April, 1955), 257-260. Fielding's great regard for Bishop Hoadly, both personally and as a theologian, is equally well attested. In *Of True Greatness* (1741) Hoadly is represented as the exemplary divine; his controversial tract, *A Plain Account of the Nature and End of the Sacrament*, is praised by Parson Adams (I, 17); and in *Tom Jones* (II, 7) his "great reputation" in divinity is remarked.

2. Tillotson, Sermon XXXIII, "Of Forgiveness of Injuries, and

Against Revenge," in *Sermons on Several Subjects and Occasions* (London, 1757), II, 403.

3. Tillotson, Sermon CCXV, "The True Remedy Against the Troubles of Life," *ibid.*, XI, 116.

4. Barrow, Sermon XL, "Keep thy Heart with All Diligence," in *Theological Works*, ed. Alexander Napier (Cambridge, 1859), III, 235.

5. Roland N. Stromberg, *Religious Liberalism in Eighteenth-Century England* (Oxford, 1954), p. 110.

6. Barrow, Sermon LII, "Of Self-Confidence, &c.," *Works*, IV, 126.

7. Barrow, Sermon VII, "The Being of God Proved from the Frame of Human Nature," *ibid.*, V, 222-226.

8. Tillotson, Sermon CXXV, "The Difficulties of a Christian Life Consider'd," *Sermons*, VII, 323.

9. Clarke, Sermon XVII, "Of the Duty of Charity," in *Sermons . . . With a Preface, giving some Account of the Life, Writings, and Character, of the Author: By Benjamin [Hoadly], Lord Bishop of Salisbury*, ed. John Clarke, 2nd ed. (London, 1730), VI, 411.

10. Clarke, Sermon XVIII, "Of Future Rewards and Punishments," *ibid.*, VII, 393.

11. Barrow, Sermon I, "The Duty and Reward of Bounty to the Poor," *Works*, I, 67; and Clarke, Sermon VI, "How to Judge of Moral Actions," *Sermons*, III, 133. In several sermons on charity, Clarke declared that the practice of this virtue was the epitome of Christianity. It was "the *Principal Part* and the *main End* of Religion" (Sermon XIII, "Of the Virtue of Charity," *ibid.*, III, 282), "the Foundation of all Religion" (Sermon XVII, "Of the Duty of Charity," *ibid.*, VI, 401), "the Summ and End of [man's] Duty" (Sermon VIII, "Of the Nature of Moral and Positive Duties," *ibid.*, VII, 173); and it "very expressively represents the *Whole of Religion*" (Sermon XVIII, "Of Future Rewards and Punishments," *ibid.*, VII, 395).

12. Hoadly, Sermon II, "Of the Divisions, and Cruelties, Falsely Imputed to Christianity," in *Sixteen Sermons Formerly Printed . . . To which are added Six Sermons upon Public Occasions* (London, 1758), p. 33.

13. Hoadly, Sermon XVI, "The Good Samaritan," *Twenty Sermons* (London, 1755), p. 337.

14. Barrow, *Works*, I, 4-5.

Notes

15. Barrow, Sermon LII, "Of Self-Confidence, &c.," *ibid.*, IV, 123.

16. Tillotson, Sermon CCIX, "Of the Necessity of Good Works," and Sermon CCX, "Of Doing All to the Glory of God," *Sermons*, XI, 17, 39.

17. Barrow, Sermon LII, "Of Self-Confidence, &c.," *Works*, IV, 123.

18. Barrow, Sermon LI, "Of Self-Love in General," *ibid.*, IV, 81.

19. Barrow, Sermon III, "The Pleasantness of Religion," *ibid.*, I, 169.

20. Hoadly, *A Plain Account of the Nature and End of the Sacrament of the Lord's Supper* (London, 1735), p. vi.

21. Tillotson, Sermon XVIII, "The Example of Jesus in Doing Good," *Sermons*, I, 424; Sermon CCIV, "Of the Form, and the Power of Godliness," *ibid.*, X, 417.

22. Clarke, Sermon XV, "Of a Future Judgment," *Sermons*, VII, 344. The doctrine of good works is maintained in countless sermons, far too many to cite.

23. *The Spectator*, No. 459, ed. George A. Aitken (London, 1898), VI, 303-304.

24. Tillotson, Sermon CCXXVIII, "The Condition of the Gospel-Covenant, and the Merit of Christ, Consistent," *Sermons*, XI, 331.

25. Aitken ed., VI, 304.

26. Hoadly, Sermon XVI, "The Good Samaritan," *Twenty Sermons*, p. 332. For Adams' phrasing of this idea, see below, p. 96.

27. Tillotson, Sermon CCVIII, "Of the Necessity of Good Works," *Sermons*, XI, 13.

28. South, Sermon V, in *Sermons Preached upon Several Occasions*, ed. William G. T. Shedd (New York, 1866-1871), IV, 63. Although a High Churchman strongly opposed to the Pelagian doctrine infiltrating the Church, South was in accord with such latitudinarians as Barrow and Tillotson in his emphasis on morality and the reasonableness of religion. Fielding mentions him in *The Champion* for November 17, December 15, 27, 1739, January 22, February 2, 14, and March 6, 1739/40. For later references to South, in whose sermons Fielding professed to find "more Wit, than in the Comedies of Congreve" (*The Covent-Garden Journal*, No. 18; Jensen ed., I, 243), consult the index to Jensen's edition of *The Covent-Garden Journal*.

29. From the start Whitefield's extreme piety, asceticism, and

A Study of *Joseph Andrews*

"enthusiasm" prompted cooler members of the Church to charge him with being "over-righteous," and in 1739 he became involved in a widely discussed pulpit duel with Dr. Joseph Trapp on the text, "Be not righteous over much"—a controversy to which Fielding amusedly alluded in *The Champion*, April 5 and May 24, 1740 (Henley ed., XV, 273, 319) and *Shamela* (Baker ed., p. 40). In replying to Trapp in "The Folly and Danger of Being Not Righteous Enough," Whitefield defended himself from the accusation of "enthusiasm and madness," insisting that we "must feel that Spirit upon our hearts" (*The Works of the Reverend George Whitefield* [London, 1771-1772], V, 125). Particularly objectionable to the advocates of common-sense and rational control, however, were the physical evidences of this "feeling the Spirit," the outward manifestations of the new birth, which broke out in the form of quaking, sighing, and convulsions during Whitefield's preaching. (Charles J. Abbey and John H. Overton, *The English Church in the Eighteenth Century* [London, 1878], I, 568.)

30. Whitefield, Sermon XXIV, "What Think Ye of Christ?," *Works*, V, 360-361.

31. Whitefield, *A Letter to the Religious Societies of England*, *ibid.*, IV, 27, 28.

32. Whitefield, Sermon XXIII, "Marks of a True Conversion," *ibid.*, V, 337.

33. Whitefield, Sermon XXXVIII, "The Indwelling of the Spirit, the Common Privilege of All Believers," *ibid.*, VI, 95.

34. Whitefield, Sermon IX, "The Folly and Danger of Being Not Righteous Enough," *ibid.*, V, 126.

35. Reported by Whitefield in "The Folly and Danger of Being Not Righteous Enough," *ibid.*, V, 135. Though he strongly denied the charge of Antinomianism, the critics can scarcely be blamed for their misinterpretation. Later in this same sermon, for example, Whitefield described his "comfortable doctrine" as follows:

> The imputed righteousness of Jesus Christ is a comfortable doctrine to all real christians; and you sinners, who ask what you must do to be saved? how uncomfortable would it be, to tell you by good works, when, perhaps, you have never done one good work in all your life: this would be driving you to despair, indeed: no; 'Believe in the Lord Jesus Christ, and you shall be saved:' therefore none of you need go away despairing. (p. 137)

Notes

III: The Good Man as Hero

1. Barrow, Sermon I, "The Duty and Reward of Bounty to the Poor," *Works*, I, 93. Compare also Sermon VI, "The Reward of Honouring God": "Only goodness is truly esteemed and honoured." (*Ibid.*, I, 265.)
2. Clarke, Sermon IX, "The Excellency of Moral Qualifications," *Sermons*, III, 189-190.
3. Steele, *The Christian Hero*, ed. Rae Blanchard (Oxford, 1932), p. 81.
4. *Ibid.*, p. 15.
5. Aitken ed., III, 380-381. Elsewhere in *The Spectator* (No. 601), those "who delight in nothing so much as in doing good, and receive more of their happiness at second-hand, or by rebound from others, than by direct and immediate sensation" are styled "these heroic souls" (*ibid.*, VIII, 194); cf. also Nos. 312 and 240, the last being a letter depicting generosity as "heroic virtue in common life" (*ibid.*, III, 345).
6. A striking illustration of how widely known and accepted the idea of the good man's heroism had become, the contest conducted by *The Gentleman's Magazine* during 1736 was to award prizes to "the 4 best Poems intitled THE CHRISTIAN HERO." (Announced in the Supplement, V [1735], 778.) In all, eight of the poems submitted were printed in the magazine for June, July, August, and September, 1736. The theatre, usually a reliable mirror of public taste and interest, provides additional evidence. *Scanderbeg: The Christian Hero* (1735), a play by Fielding's friend George Lillo, was a dismal attempt to dramatize the concept.
7. Tillotson, Sermon CI, "Of the Work Assign'd to Every Man, and the Season for Doing It," *Sermons*, VI, 283.
8. Hoadly, Sermon XIV, "The Nature of the Kingdom, or Church, of Christ," *Sixteen Sermons*, p. 286. With Tillotson and Hoadly compare Samuel Clarke, who declared that the good man is marked by "*in general* a *virtuous* Life, but who moreover is *particularly* eminent for *Benignity* of Temper." (Sermon IX, "The Excellency of Moral Qualifications," *Sermons*, III, 198-199.)
9. Barrow, Sermon I, *Works*, I, 18, 19.
10. Barrow, Sermon XXVII, *ibid.*, II, 314-315.
11. Tillotson, Sermon LXVIII, "Good Men Strangers and Sojourners upon Earth," *Sermons*, V, 166-168.

12. Clarke, Sermon IV, *Sermons*, III, 86.

13. Clarke, Sermon XI, *ibid.*, II, 254; see also pp. 243, 248-249.

14. Barrow, Sermon III, *Works*, V, 108; South, Sermon LXIV, *Sermons*, III, 356-357.

15. The Joseph story was, of course, familiar to Fielding's contemporaries. For example, in "An Apology for the Censorious," a slight poem in defense of Pamela's virtue appearing in *The London Magazine*, X (July, 1741), 358, the author rebukes those who ridicule male chastity:

> Thus, on *Joseph* the patriarch's detesting
> The thought of *adulterous* stains,
> They forbear not (forsooth!) their rude jesting,
> But term him *a fool* for his pains.

Notice, too, the verse essay "On Joseph and Potiphar's Wife" in *The Gentleman's Magazine*, XVIII (May, 1748), 231. Most interesting, however, is the use to which the story was put on the Continent, where it had long been a favorite with the writers of the biblical epic. (See below, note 30.)

As for Fielding, in addition to the references in *Joseph Andrews*, he later used the chastity of Joseph as a foil to Booth's incontinence in *Amelia* (X, 2): "Though not absolutely a Joseph . . . yet could he not be guilty of premeditated inconstancy." (Henley ed., VII, 193.)

16. Some time ago a contributor to *Notes and Queries* pointed out the curious correspondence between the names of several of Fielding's characters—among them Joseph Andrews and Abraham Adams—and those of certain subscribers to Bishop Burnet's *History of His Own Time* (folio, 1724-1734). (Y. Y., "Names of Characters in Fielding's Novels," *N&Q*, 9th Ser., II [November 26, 1898], 426.) Although the list is quite inclusive, the names are in general too commonplace for one to determine whether the similarity is coincidental, as Cross believes (I, 342), or deliberate, as I. P. Watt suspects ("The Naming of Characters in Defoe, Richardson, and Fielding," *RES*, XXV [1949], 335).

17. Fielding, it will be recalled, conceived of his novels not only as prose epics, but also as "histories" or "biographies." See *Joseph Andrews* (III, 1) and Robert M. Wallace, "Fielding's Knowledge of History and Biography," *SP*, XLIV (1947), 89-107.

18. Barrow, *Works*, II, 499, 520.

Notes

19. *Ibid.*, II, 500.
20. *Ibid.*, II, 498-499.
21. *Ibid.*, II, 501.
22. *Ibid.*, II, 501-503.
23. *Ibid.*, II, 504.
24. *Ibid.*, II, 520.
25. *Ibid.*, II, 521-522.
26. *Ibid.*, II, 522.
27. *Ibid.*, II, 513.

28. Henley ed., IV, 195-196. Barrow, of course, was neither the only nor the most likely source for the theory of the virtuous but imperfect hero. Le Bossu, Fielding's favorite critic among the moderns, had popularized the concept in his *Traité du poëme epique,* and he was followed by Dryden, Blackmore, and Dennis, among others. (See H. T. Swedenberg, *The Theory of the Epic in England, 1650-1800*, University of California Publications in English, Vol. XV [Berkeley, 1944], pp. 24, 306-307.)

29. Sayce, *The French Biblical Epic in the Seventeenth Century* (Oxford, 1955), p. 181.

30. Sayce (pp. 257-258) cites the following: Fracastorius, *Joseph* (1555); Lodovico Dolce, *La Vita di Giuseppe* (1561); Saint-Peres, *La Vie de Joseph* (1648); Saint-Amant, *Joseph* (1658); Julien-Gatien Morillon, *Joseph, ou l'esclave fidele* (1679); and Jean Desmarets de Saint-Sorlin, *Abraham, ou la vie parfaite* (1680).

31. In J. E. Spingarn, ed., *Critical Essays of the Seventeenth Century* (Oxford, 1908), II, 88, 90.

32. See *The Covent-Garden Journal*, No. 19 (March 7, 1752), *Tom Jones* (IX,1), and *Joseph Andrews* (II, 1). Earlier in the *Vernoniad*, along with his mock imitation of Virgil, Fielding had burlesqued the style and machinery of *Paradise Lost*. We may infer Fielding's acknowledgment of the superior moral purpose of *Paradise Lost* as a Christian epic. In *The Covent-Garden Journal*, No. 24 (March 24, 1752), for example, he praised Milton's championing of "the great Cause of Christianity." (Jensen ed., I, 279.) At the time of *A Journey from this World to the Next* (I, 9), furthermore, he had objected to Dryden's claim that Satan, and not Adam, was the hero of *Paradise Lost* (Henley ed., II, 249). Even more significant is Fielding's likening Tom Jones to Adam expelled from Paradise (*Tom Jones*, VII, 2; see below, p. 90).

A Study of *Joseph Andrews*

Though it places him on the side of Boileau against Milton's practice (in this instance at least), Fielding's refusal to allow the Christian writer to use supernatural machinery—except for ghosts—is further evidence that he was familiar with contemporary theories of the Christian epic (*Tom Jones*, VIII, 1). See Swedenberg, p. 266, and Thornbury, pp. 143-144.

33. See Willey's tenth chapter, "The Heroic Poem in a Scientific Age," *The Seventeenth Century Background: Studies in the Thought of the Age in Relation to Poetry and Religion* (London, 1934).

34. See, for instance, Woodford's Preface to *A Paraphrase upon the Psalms of David* (1667); Dryden's *A Discourse Concerning the Original and Progress of Satire* (1693); Blackmore's Preface to *Prince Arthur* (1695); Dennis' *The Advancement and Reformation of Modern Poetry* (1701) and *The Grounds of Criticism in Poetry* (1704); and Watts' Preface to *Horae Lyricae* (1706).

35. Swedenberg, pp. 149-150.

36. Tillyard, *The English Epic and Its Background* (London, 1954), pp. 376-377. Tillyard quotes the following passage from William Haller's *The Rise of Puritanism*:

> The Puritan imagination saw the life of the spirit as pilgrimage and battle. The images of wayfaring and warfaring which fill the Old Testament had been exploited by that fighting itinerant, Paul, and by generations upon generations of subsequent evangelists. Reaching the pulpits of the seventeenth century by a hundred channels, they there underwent new and peculiarly vigorous development. [The Christian] was a traveler through a strange country and a soldier in battle. He was a traveler who, fleeing from destruction, must adhere through peril and hardship to the way that leads home. He was a soldier who, having been pressed to serve under the banners of the spirit, must enact faithfully his part in the unceasing war of the spiritual against the carnal man.

37. Barrow, Sermon XXXVII, *Works*, III, 85-86. Barrow repeats the idea in Sermon III, "Of the Virtue and Reasonableness of Faith," where the life of the good man is "merely wayfaring, in passage toward his true home and heavenly country" (*ibid.*, V, 103).

38. Hoadly, Sermon VIII, *Twenty Sermons*, pp. 149-150.

39. Clarke, Sermon IV, *Sermons*, III, 85.

40. Tillotson, Sermon LXVIII, *Sermons*, V, 168, 176.

Notes

IV: Vanity, Fortune, and the Classical Ideal

1. Reed, *The Background of Gray's "Elegy": A Study in the Taste for Melancholy Poetry, 1700-1751*, Columbia University Studies in English and Comparative Literature, Vol. 35 (New York, 1924), pp. 125-126.

2. Prior's Preface to *Solomon on the Vanity of the World*, in *Poems on Several Occasions*, ed. A.R. Waller (Cambridge, 1905), p. 256.

3. Barrow, Sermon XLI, "The Consideration of Our Latter End," *Works*, III, 251.

4. There are several excellent studies of the abundant seventeenth- and eighteenth-century literature on this theme. The following are perhaps the most useful: Reed, pp. 33-225; Raymond D. Havens, "Solitude and the Neoclassicists," *ELH*, XXI (1954), 251-273; and Maren-Sofie Røstvig, *The Happy Man: Studies in the Metamorphoses of a Classical Ideal, 1600-1760*, Oslo Studies in English, Nos. 2, 7 (Oslo, 1954, 1958), 2 vols. In his informative chapter "The Classical Ideal of Life in Poetry," Calvin D. Yost has noticed the popularity of the theme in *The Gentleman's Magazine*. (*The Poetry of the "Gentleman's Magazine" : A Study in Eighteenth Century Literary Taste* [Philadelphia, 1936].)

5. J. E. Congleton, *Theories of Pastoral Poetry in England, 1684-1798* (Gainesville, Florida, 1952), p. 174. For a useful account of the Golden Age and pastoral poetry, consult *The Guardian*, No. 22 (April 6, 1713).

6. Barrow, Sermon V, "The Profitableness of Godliness," *Works*, I, 211. Elsewhere Barrow remarks, "Fools may dream of, but no wise man could ever find a paradise in this world." (Sermon XLI, "The Consideration of Our Latter End," *ibid.*, III, 248, n.)

7. South, Sermon XLVII, "Covetousness an Absurdity in Reason and a Contradiction to Religion," *Sermons*, II, 508. See also Sermon XIII, "The Practice of Religion Enforced by Reason," *ibid.*, I, 268-269.

8. South, Sermon LVIII, "The Nature, Causes, and Consequences of Envy," *ibid.*, III, 228. Unlike the poets, who were operating within a prescribed literary convention, the clergy were not customarily so much concerned with recommending any one particular course of life as with defining the components of happiness in any condition; and they were anxious lest, in retirement, the individual

A Study of *Joseph Andrews*

should neglect his duty to society. Like the Stoic philosophers, Barrow could praise the solitude of the pious man as affording an opportunity for contemplation and introspection. ("The Profitableness of Godliness," *Works*, I, 231-232.) Typically, though, the divines merely defined contentment as consisting of a competency of worldly goods, submission to the will of God, and a continuing course of virtue and temperance.

9. Hoadly, Sermon XIV, "The Different Characters of John the Baptist, and Jesus Christ," *Twenty Sermons*, pp. 289-290.

10. South, Sermon VIII, "All Contingencies under the Direction of God's Providence," *Sermons*, I, 147.

11. Clarke, Sermon XVI, "That Every Man Shall Finally Receive According to His Works," *Sermons*, VII, 365. A. R. Towers has indicated that a likely source for the *Amelia* passage is in Clarke's Boyle Lectures for 1705. (*MLN*, LXX [1955], 258-260.) The quotation I have chosen is an additional instance of the same idea.

12. Barrow, Sermon I, "The Duty and Reward of Bounty to the Poor," *Works*, I, 75-76. South devoted an entire sermon to the subject: Sermon XXXVIII, "Prosperity Ever Dangerous to Virtue," *Sermons*, II.

13. Clarke, Sermon XII, "The End of God's Afflicting Men," *Sermons*, VI, 277-278.

14. Barrow, Sermon XXXVII, "Of Contentment," *Works*, III, 62-63.

15. *Ibid.*, III, 66. Cf. South regarding "the sharp trials of adversity: which yet God uses as the most proper and sovereign means to correct and reduce a soul grown vain and extravagant, by a long, uninterrupted felicity." (Sermon XXXVIII, "Prosperity Ever Dangerous to Virtue," *Sermons*, II, 305.)

16. Clarke, Sermon X, "The Shortness and Vanity of Humane Life," *Sermons*, VI, 242-243.

V: Fielding's Ethics

1. Henley ed., XV, 279.

2. Mack, "The Muse of Satire," *Yale Review*, XLI (1951), 88-90.

3. Irwin, *The Making of "Jonathan Wild": A Study in the Literary Method of Henry Fielding* (New York, 1941), p. 69.

Notes

4. *The Spectator*, No. 177 (September 22, 1711).

5. *The Champion* (January 22, 1739/40); Henley ed., XV, 162.

6. *The Champion* (December 11, 1739); Henley ed., XV, 94. In his Preface to the *Miscellanies*, Fielding similarly objects to those "very shameless writers" who consider "Newgate as no other than human nature with its mask off": "For my part, I understand those writers who describe human nature in this depraved character, as speaking only of such persons as Wild and his gang; and I think it may be justly inferred, that they do not find in their own bosoms any deviation from the general rule." (Henley ed., XII, 243.) *The True Patriot*, No. 17 (February 18-25, 1746), is equally emphatic:

> Every one who searches his own rotten Heart, and finds not a Grain of Goodness in it, very easily persuades himself, that there is none in any other. This he proclaims aloud, and all those under the same Predicament as readily subscribe to his Opinion.

7. Henley ed., III, 270-271.

8. See *The Covent-Garden Journal*, No. 21 (March 14, 1752).

9. *Amelia*, III, 5; Henley ed., VI, 127-128. Earlier in *Amelia* (I, 2) Fielding had described the thoroughly corrupt Justice Thrasher as an egregious example of "that fundamental principle so strongly laid down in the institutes of the learned Rochefoucault, by which the duty of self-love is so strongly enforced, and every man is taught to consider himself as the centre of gravity, and to attract all things thither" (Henley ed., VI, 17).

10. Henley ed., IV, 152.

11. Sherburn, "Fielding's Social Outlook," *PQ*, XXXV (1956), 7-16.

12. See Swann, pp. 59-64.

13. Henley ed., XV, 94.

14. *The Champion* (March 6, 1739/40); Henley ed., XV, 233. When he was penniless and looking for work as a "Hackney-writer," Mr. Wilson was contemned by his associates. He later observes to Parson Adams that "there is a Malignity in the Nature of Man, which, when not weeded out, or at least covered by a good Education and Politeness, delights in making another uneasy or dissatisfied with himself" (III, 3).

15. *A Clear State of the Case of Elizabeth Canning* (1753);

A Study of *Joseph Andrews*

Henley ed., XIII, 230. Despite his belief in the essential goodness of human nature, Dr. Harrison recognizes as well a darker side; the practice of slander, he declares, is rooted in "the malicious disposition of mankind . . . and the cruel pleasure which [men] take in destroying the reputations of others." (*Amelia*, III, 1; Henley ed., VI, 109.)

16. *The Champion* (December 25, 1739); Henley ed., XV, 116. Compare, too, these humorous lines from *A Description of U—n G—* (*Alias New Hog's Norton*): "Happy for us, had Eve's this garden been;/ She'd found no fruit, and therefore known no sin." (Henley ed., XII, 278.)

17. Henley ed., XII, 275.

18. Henley ed., II, 238.

19. *An Essay on the Knowledge of the Characters of Men*, Henley ed., XIV, 282. We may also recall the dispute between Joseph Andrews and Parson Adams over the efficacy of education in correcting vicious inclinations: "I remember when I was in the Stable," Joseph remarks, "if a young Horse was vicious in his Nature, no Correction would make him otherwise: I take it to be equally the same among Men: if a Boy be of a mischievous wicked Inclination, no School, though ever so private, will ever make him good: on the contrary, if he be of a righteous Temper, you may trust him to London, or wherever else you please, he will be in no danger of being corrupted" (III, 5).

20. *Amelia*, XII, 5; Henley ed., VII, 313.

21. Henley ed., XV, 178.

22. *Amelia*, IX, 5; Henley ed., VII, 145. For Barrow's position, see above, p. 16.

23. Henley ed., XIII, 110.

24. Jensen ed., I, 308.

25. *An Essay on Conversation*, Henley ed., XIV, 247.

26. *Tom Jones*, IV, 6; Henley ed., III, 164.

27. *Amelia*, IX, 4; Henley ed., VII, 142.

28. *The Journal of a Voyage to Lisbon*, Henley ed., XVI, 201.

29. Henley ed., XV, 260.

30. Jensen ed., I, 232-233.

31. *The Covent-Garden Journal*, No. 29 (April 11, 1752); Jensen ed., I, 309.

32. Henley ed., VII, 167-168. Compare the earlier Shaftesburian

Notes

correlation between an esthetic and a moral sense in Letter XL, which Fielding had contributed to his sister's *Familiar Letters*:

> There is a strict analogy between taste and morals of an age; and depravity in the one always induces depravity in the other. True taste is indeed no other than the knowledge of what is right and fit in every thing. (Henley ed., XVI, 28-29.)

Though Fielding very probably is recalling Shaftesbury in these passages, he could have found the roots of the idea in the latitudinarians. Consider Barrow's Sermon XXVIII, "Of the Love of Our Neighbour": "The practice of benignity, of courtesy, of clemency ... [is] no less grateful and amiable to the mind, than beauty to our eyes, harmony to our ears, fragrancy to our smell, and sweetness to our palate: and to the same mental sense, malignity, cruelty, harshness, all kinds of uncharitable dealing are very disgustful and loathsome." (*Works*, II, 328-329.) Statements of the existence of an intuitive sense recognizing absolute good and evil, right and wrong, occur as well in Tillotson, South, and Clarke. Fielding's view, like that of the divines, was more usually that of an innate conscience—"those secret institutions, which God hath written in the heart and conscience of every man." (*Examples of the Interposition of Providence*, Henley ed., XVI, 119.)

33. *The Champion* (March 13, 1739/40); Henley ed., XV, 241.

34. Amelia's manner of educating her children is a clear representation of Fielding's views. By discipline and the daily inculcation of lessons of religion and morality, she had encouraged their benevolent inclinations and greatly suppressed any vicious tendencies:

> This admirable woman never let a day pass without instructing her children in some lesson of religion and morality. By which means she had, in their tender minds, so strongly annexed the ideas of fear and shame to every idea of evil of which they were susceptible, that it must require great pains and length of habit to separate them. Though she was the tenderest of mothers, she never suffered any symptom of malevolence to show itself in their most trifling actions without discouragement, without rebuke, and, if it broke forth with any rancor, without punishment. In which she had such success, that not the least marks of pride, envy, malice, or spite discovered itself in any of their little words or deeds. (*Amelia*, IV, 3; Henley ed., VI, 191.)

35. *The Covent-Garden Journal*, No. 48 (June 16, 1752); Jensen ed., II, 27.

36. *The Covent-Garden Journal*, No. 56 (July 25, 1752); Jensen ed., II, 65.

37. Henley ed., V, 141.

38. *The Champion* (March 4, 1739/40); Henley ed., XV, 230. Similar reasoning consoled Tom Jones, unjustly charged with the "murder" of Mr. Fitzpatrick. (*Tom Jones*, XVII, 9.)

39. *Amelia*, XII, 5; Henley ed., VII, 313.

40. *A Proposal for Making an Effectual Provision for the Poor*, Henley ed., XIII, 186.

41. Henley ed., V, 33.

42. Henley ed., XII, 258-259.

43. *An Essay on the Knowledge of the Characters of Men*, Henley ed., XIV, 285.

44. Cf. Fielding's views in *The Remedy of Affliction for the Loss of Our Friends*.

45. Henley ed., VII, 113.

46. Jensen ed., I, 306-307.

47. *Tom Jones*, XIV, 6; Henley ed., V, 115. *Amelia*, VIII, 5; Henley ed., VII, 90.

48. Henley ed., XIII, 109. The importance of empathy to the psychology of good nature is further indicated by the following statement of Mr. Boncour, the hero of Fielding's posthumously published comedy, *The Fathers; or, The Good-Natured Man*:

> How wretched is that animal, whose whole happiness centres in himself; who cannot feel any satisfaction, but in the indulgence of his own appetite. I feel my children still a part of me; they are, as it were, additional senses, which let in daily a thousand pleasures to me. (Henley ed., XII, 166-167.)

49. *Tom Jones*, I, 3; Henley ed., III, 26. Compare Fielding's description of Mrs. Heartfree's good nature: "A benevolence which is an emanation from the heart." (*Jonathan Wild*, II, 1; Henley ed., II, 53.)

50. Henley ed., XV, 136.

51. Henley ed., XIII, 109.

52. *Tom Jones*, III, 4; Henley ed., III, 118. Italics mine.

53. Quoted in Cross, II, 246.

Notes

54. *Tom Jones*, XII, 10; Henley ed., IV, 346.
55. *ELH*, I (1934), 228.
56. Jensen ed., II, 9. Earlier in the *Journal*, No. 16 (February 25, 1752), this hedonistic strain of sentimentalism was revealed in the self-analysis of Axylus, one of Fielding's good-natured men:

> It is natural for the Mind of Man to hunt after those Objects in which it takes Delight, and to shun those which give it Pain. . . . Whenever I can by my Company, by my Advice, or by my Purse, relieve the Solitary, the Simple, or the Distressed, I never fail of doing it; and when my Endeavours are crowned with Success, I enjoy a most exquisite Pleasure. (Jensen ed., I, 234.)

57. Jensen ed., I, 308.
58. Henley ed., XV, 217.
59. Henley ed., XIV, 283.
60. *An Inquiry into the Causes of the Late Increase of Robbers*, Henley ed., XIII, 110-111. Fielding recognized the danger of being, like Heartfree, "good-natured, friendly, and generous to a great excess" (*Jonathan Wild*, II, 1; Henley ed., II, 52).
61. Jensen ed., II, 10. See also *The Champion* (February 16, 1739/40) and *The Jacobite's Journal*, Nos. 31 and 32 (July 2, 9, 1748).
62. *Amelia*, III, 1; Henley ed., VI, 111. If this distinctive insistence upon a judicious selection of the objects of benevolence be remembered, Fielding's over-all approval of the school of sentiment may be acknowledged. In *Amelia* (IX, 4), his final novel and closer in tone to Richardson than any of its predecessors, he thus observes that Captain Booth "had a tenderness of heart which is rarely found among men; for which I know no other reason than that true goodness is rarely found among them; for I am firmly persuaded that the latter never possessed any human mind in any degree without being attended by as large a portion of the former." (Henley ed., VII, 142.) And in *Tom Jones* (VI, 5), Sophia defends her reading of a sentimental novel: "I love a tender sensation . . . and would pay the price of a tear for it at any time." (Henley ed., III, 288.)
63. *The True Patriot*, No. 8 (December 24, 1745).
64. Henley ed., XV, 258.
65. Henley ed., XV, 259.

66. *Tom Jones*, XVIII, 11; Henley ed., V, 358.

67. *An Inquiry into the Causes of the Late Increase of Robbers*, Henley ed., XIII, 119. Fittingly enough, Fielding revealed his own ability to make "the distinction between an object of mercy, and an object of justice," when as magistrate he condemned Bosavern Penlez and acquitted one Wilson, "whose case to me seemed to be the object of true compassion." (*A True State of the Case of Bosavern Penlez*, Henley ed., XIII, 288.)

68. Henley ed., XV, 259-260.

69. Henley ed., XV, 260.

70. *An Essay on the Knowledge of the Characters of Men*, Henley ed., XIV, 286.

71. Jensen ed., I, 232.

72. *Tom Jones*, IV, 6, and XV, 1; Henley ed., III, 164, and V, 141. Unless translated into action, mere good-natured pity is a fraud. In one of his earliest comedies, *Don Quixote in England* (1733), Fielding thus has his hero remark to Sancho:

> What is a good-natured man? Why, one who, seeing the want of his friend, cries, he pities him! Is this real? No: if it was he would relieve him. His pity is triumphant arrogance and insult; it arises from his pride, not from his compassion. (Henley ed., XI, 32)

73. *An Essay on the Knowledge of the Characters of Men*, Henley ed., XIV, 293.

74. Henley ed., XV, 258. Later, in defining the necessary qualifications of the true clergyman, Fielding insists upon the forgiveness of one's enemies: such forgiveness "is the characteristic of a Christian minister, and must distinguish him from the best of the heathens, who taught no such doctrine." (*The Champion* [April 5, 1740]; Henley ed., XV, 270.)

75. *The Covent-Garden Journal*, No. 39 (May 16, 1752); Jensen ed., I, 357.

76. *The Covent-Garden Journal*, No. 2 (January 7, 1752); Jensen ed., I, 143.

77. Henley ed., XV, 204.

78. *The Covent-Garden Journal*, No. 44 (June 2, 1752); Jensen ed., II, 9.

Notes

79. *The Covent-Garden Journal*, No. 21 (March 14, 1752); Jensen ed., I, 261-262. *The Champion* (April 5, 1740); Henley ed., XV, 269.

80. *The Covent-Garden Journal*, No. 29 (April 11, 1752); Jensen ed., I, 305.

81. *The Champion* (April 5, 1740); Henley ed., XV, 270.

82. Henley ed., III, 81-83. Fielding's personal generosity is well attested by his chief biographer. As manager of the Haymarket Theatre, he devoted the proceeds of several benefits to the relief of persons in distress (Cross, I, 198), and he long contributed to the support of his sisters and of Margaret and Jane Collier, whom he knew from childhood (*ibid.*, III, 272). His charities, in fact, often exceeded his means. While editing *The Covent-Garden Journal*, for example, he organized a subscription—to which he contributed a guinea, as much as Lyttelton and twice as much as Warburton—for a burned-out Bloomsbury baker named Peirce. On another occasion he collected a smaller purse for one Redman, a distressed shopkeeper. He was as well a "perpetual governor" of the Lying-in Hospital for married women, an office that probably cost him thirty guineas (*ibid.*, II, 302-303). As a justice, he virtually impoverished himself by striving to correct miscreants instead of completing their ruin by committing them to prison, for when there was no commitment, there was no fee (*ibid.*, II, 301-302); and in an effort to curb the steady increase of crime, he distributed gratis his *Examples of the Interposition of Providence in the Detection and Punishment of Murder* (*ibid.*, II, 270).

83. Murphy, "An Essay on the Life and Genius of Henry Fielding, Esq.," *Works*, 3rd ed. (London, 1766), I, 51.

84. Henley ed., XII, 238.

85. *Journey*, I, 7; Henley ed., II, 244, 245.

86. In one of his reincarnations (I, 20), Julian was killed at birth and had to be born again. That Fielding, believing in the attainment of virtue through the shaping powers of reason and free will, conceived of the individual as earning salvation by the exercise of charity is clearly implied by Julian's comment: "Spirits, who end their lives before they are at the age of five years are immediately ordered into other bodies." (Henley ed., II, 298.) Fielding's position here is analogous to the Pelagian doctrine contradicted, for example, by the Middle English poem, *The Pearl*, a work of course unknown to him. Orthodox Christianity asserted the efficacy of in-

Notes

fant baptism, while Pelagianism maintained that salvation was achieved through the *responsible* performance of good works.
  87. Jensen ed., I, 358.
  88. Jensen ed., I, 309.
  89. Jensen ed., II, 9.
  90. *Jonathan Wild*, IV, 1; Henley ed., II, 144.
  91. *Tom Jones*, IV, 4; Henley ed., III, 154.
  92. *Amelia*, IX, 8; Henley ed., VII, 162.
  93. Baker ed., p. 40. For an informative discussion of Fielding's satire against Whitefield and Methodism in *Shamela*, consult Baker's introduction, pp. xvi-xxi.
  94. Henley ed., IV, 92-93.
  95. Henley ed., V, 371.
  96. Henley ed., VI, 30.

VI: The Novel: Meaning and Structure

  1. Compare the following incidents, for example: 1. the night adventure in the inn involving Don Quixote, Maritornes, and the mule driver *with* the confusion in Madam Slipslop's bedchamber (*DQ*, I, 16; *JA*, IV, 14); 2. Maritornes' charity to Sancho *with* that of Betty the chambermaid to Joseph (*DQ*, I, 17; *JA*, I, 13); 3. Don Quixote and Sancho's frightened bewilderment at the strange lights of the funeral cortege *with* the reaction of Adams, Joseph, and Fanny to the lights of the sheepstealers (*DQ*, I, 19; *JA*, III, 2); 4. Clara's recognition of her lover by the sweetness of his singing *with* the reunion of Fanny and Joseph (*DQ*, I, 42-43; *JA*, II, 12); and 5. the series of practical jokes that the Duke and Duchess play on Don Quixote and Sancho *with* the treatment of Adams at the hands of the "roasting" squire (*DQ*, II, 31ff.; *JA*, III, 7).
  2. Dudden, I, 351, and II, 1101.
  3. *The Covent-Garden Journal*, No. 24 (March 24, 1752); Jensen ed., I, 281.
  4. Henley ed., XVI, 11; italics mine.
  5. Digeon, pp. 161-162.
  6. *PQ*, XXXV (1956), 1.
  7. Le Bossu, *Traité du poëme epique* (Paris, 1675), p. 14. Fielding has high praise for Le Bossu, placing him in the same company with Aristotle, Horace, and Longinus. (*Tom Jones*, XI, 1.)

Notes

8. See Swedenberg, pp. 193-194. The place of allegory in eighteenth-century criticism is discussed in Edward A. Bloom's useful article, "The Allegorical Principle," *ELH*, XVIII (1951), 163-190.

9. In his excellent introduction to the Rinehart edition (New York, 1952), Maynard Mack has noticed that "the two poles of value in *Joseph Andrews* (as later in *Tom Jones*) are the country-world and the city, neither perfect, but the former superior to the latter because more honest" (p. xii).

10. On Fielding's use of the *Aeneid* in his final novel, see George Sherburn, "Fielding's *Amelia*: An Interpretation," *ELH*, III (1936), 2-4, and Lyall H. Powers, "The Influence of the *Aeneid* on Fielding's *Amelia*," *MLN*, LXXI (May, 1956), 330-336. Fielding, for example, seems to have modeled the affair between Booth and Miss Matthews in Newgate on that between Aeneas and Dido in the cave. Ian Watt's observations on this episode may be applied as well to Fielding's method in *Joseph Andrews*, where, however, the parallels are more accessible and apparent: "This kind of analogy involves no more than a kind of narrative metaphor which assists the imagination of the writer to find a pattern for his own observation of life without in any way detracting from the novel's appearance of literal veracity." (*The Rise of the Novel : Studies in Defoe, Richardson and Fielding* [London, 1957], p. 255.)

11. *Tom Jones*, VII, 2; Henley ed., III, 337.

12. *Tom Jones*, XVIII, 13; Henley ed., V, 373.

13. For a discussion of the theme of Joseph's coming of age, see Dick Taylor, Jr., "Joseph as Hero of *Joseph Andrews*," *Tulane Studies in English*, VII (1957), 91-109.

14. *PQ*, XXXV (1956), 10.

15. Henley ed., VIII, 52.

16. Henley ed., IX, 163.

17. *Of True Greatness*, Henley ed., XII, 254.

18. *The Covent-Garden Journal*, No. 11 (February 8, 1752); Jensen ed., I, 202.

19. Henley ed., XII, 62, 63. Compare Lady Bellaston's remark to Lord Fellamar:

> "Consider the country—the bane of all young women is the country. There they learn a set of romantic notions of love, and I know not what folly, which this town and good company can

scarce eradicate in a whole winter." (*Tom Jones*, XV, 2; Henley ed., V, 146.)

20. Henley ed., III, 169.

21. *Tom Jones*, I, 1; Henley ed., III, 19.

22. The tradesman Heartfree in *Jonathan Wild* is an apparent exception, but even he recognizes the wisdom of this ideal. Unjustly imprisoned, Heartfree voices his conviction of the vanity of worldly pursuits and recommends the solution adopted by the Wilsons:

> "But let us survey those whose understandings are of a more elevated and refined temper; how empty do they soon find the world of enjoyments worth their desire or attaining! How soon do they retreat to solitude and contemplation, to gardening and planting, and such rural amusements, where their trees and they enjoy the air and the sun in common, and both vegetate with very little difference between them." (III, 2; Henley ed., II, 100-101.)

23. Henley ed., VI, 167.

24. See Adams' letter to *The True Patriot*, No. 7 (December 17, 1745).

25. Joseph reveals to Pamela that, the moment he is discharged by Lady Booby, he "shall return to my old Master's Country-Seat, if it be only to see Parson Adams, who is the best Man in the World" (I, 6).

26. Sermon XVI, "The Good Samaritan," *Twenty Sermons*, p. 323. The parable, Hoadly remarks, was designed to teach "that strict Bond of *Nature*, by which all Men are allied to one another" (p. 318), and that one's neighbor is "every Person in the World, of what *Country*, of what *Profession*, of what *Religion* soever, who is in Necessity, and stands in Need of your Assistance, and whom you can assist without *Injury* to *Yourself*, or to Those for whom you are more nearly concerned; That every such Man has a *Title* to your *Beneficence* and *Charity*" (pp. 321-322). Similarly, Isaac Barrow cites the example of the Samaritan, "whence it might appear, that this relation of neighbourhood is universal and unlimited." (Sermon XXVII, "Of the Love of Our Neighbour," *Works*, II, 300.)

27. It is notable how often Fielding's Samaritans may be found among the lower classes of society. In *Joseph Andrews*, besides the

Notes

postilion and Betty, we may recall the fellow servant who clothed Joseph at the start of his journey (I, 10) and the pedlar who gave his last penny to enable Adams to discharge his account with the alehouse hostess (II, 15) and who later rescued the parson's son from drowning (IV, 8). One explanation may well be disclosed in Booth's remark to Amelia: "Compassion, if thoroughly examined, will, I believe, appear to be the fellow-feeling only of men of the same rank and degree of life for one another, on account of the evils to which they themselves are liable." (*Amelia*, X, 9; Henley ed., VII, 236.)

28. See above, p. 22.

29. Hoadly, *A Plain Account of the Nature and End of the Sacrament*, p. 157.

30. Henley ed., XV, 245.

31. This species of easy verbal charity received Fielding's special attention in *An Essay on the Knowledge of the Characters of Men*, Henley ed., XIV, 293. Isaac Barrow called this character "a *Doson*, or *Will-give*" and contrasted him severely to the truly charitable man who actively works to relieve the distresses of others. (Sermon I, "The Duty and Reward of Bounty to the Poor," *Works*, I, 10.)

32. Barrow's words are as follows:

> We should be always, in affection and disposition of mind, ready to part with anything we have for the succour of our poor brethren; that to the utmost of our ability (according to moral estimation prudently rated) upon all occasions we should really express that disposition in our practice; that we are exceedingly obliged to the continual exercise of these duties in a very eminent degree. (*Works*, I, 14)

33. Joseph's remarks are in substance quite close to a passage in Barrow's "The Duty and Reward of Bounty to the Poor," *Works*, I, 90-94. Barrow's aim is to show that true honor is the reward of charity, not wealth or fashionableness. (See above, p. 27.)

34. *The Gray's-Inn Journal*, No. 96 (August 17, 1754).

35. Only if we credit Hobbes' narrow notion that all laughter is an expression of contempt can we mistake Adams for the object of his author's derision. It is instructive to keep in mind George Meredith's observation: "You may estimate your capacity for comic

perception by being able to detect the ridicule of them you love without loving them less." Meredith continues by distinguishing between the modes of Satire, Irony, and Humor, the last of which he describes as follows: "If you laugh all round [the ridiculous person], tumble him, roll him about, deal him a smack, and drop a tear on him, own his likeness to you, and yours to your neighbor, spare him as little as you shun, pity him as much as you expose, it is a spirit of Humor that is moving you." "Parson Adams," he declares, "is a creation of humor." ("An Essay on Comedy," in *Comedy*, intro. Wylie Sypher [New York: Doubleday Anchor Books, 1956], pp. 42-43.)

36. *The Covent-Garden Journal*, No. 55 (July 18, 1752); Jensen ed., II, 63.

37. Samuel Clarke, Sermon IV, "The Character of a Good Man," *Sermons*, III, 86.

38. *The Champion* (March 29, 1740); Henley ed., XV, 263.

39. *The Champion* (April 12, 1740); Henley ed., XV, 274.

40. *The Champion* (April 19, 1740); Henley ed., XV, 283.

41. Henley ed., XV, 222.

42. In *The Champion* (April 5, 1740), Fielding similarly insisted on "poverty" as the final qualification of the true clergyman, and, by reference to the Trapp-Whitefield controversy, indicated that his sympathies—in this respect at least—were with the Methodist: "Without being righteous over-much, we may, I think, conclude, that if the clergy are not to abandon all they have to their ministry, neither are they to get immense estates by it; and I would recommend it to the consideration of those who do, whether they do not make a trade of divinity?" (Henley ed., XV, 273.)

43. Fielding clearly intended this well-known incident to recall Genesis XXII: 1-18, the account of the sacrifice of Isaac. Adams advises Joseph that "we must submit in all things to the Will of Providence, and not set our Affections so much on anything here as not to be able to quit it without Reluctance." Then, as preparation for the analogy shortly to follow, he remarks: "Had Abraham so loved his Son Isaac as to refuse the Sacrifice required, is there any of us who would not condemn him?" (IV, 8).

44. The good parson's dedication to his office, his unwillingness to profane his calling by truckling to the whims of his superiors, is nowhere better demonstrated than on the occasion of the marriage of Joseph and Fanny. At church, Fielding observes:

Notes

Nothing was so remarkable as the extraordinary and unaffected Modesty of Fanny, unless the true Christian Piety of Adams, who publickly rebuked Mr. Booby and Pamela for laughing in so sacred a Place, and so solemn an Occasion. Our Parson would have done no less to the highest Prince on Earth; for, though he paid all Submission and Deference to his Superiours in other Matters, where the least Spice of Religion intervened he immediately lost all Respect of Persons. It was his Maxim, that he was a Servant of the Highest, and could not, without departing from his Duty, give up the least Article of his Honour or of his Cause to the greatest earthly Potentate. Indeed, he always asserted that Mr. Adams at Church with his Surplice on, and Mr. Adams without that Ornament in any other place, were two very different Persons. (IV, 16)

45. Booth "had a tenderness of heart which is rarely found among men; for which I know no other reason than that true goodness is rarely found among them; for I am firmly persuaded that the latter never possessed any human mind in any degree without being attended by as large a portion of the former." (*Amelia*, IX, 4; Henley ed., VII, 142.)

46. *The Champion* (March 27, 1740); Henley ed., XV, 259.

47. It was only natural that Fielding should fashion Parson Adams, the incarnation of good nature, after the model of Don Quixote. As early as *The Coffee-House Politician* (1730), Fielding tended to identify good nature and quixotism. Consider, for instance, Constant's soliloquy:

> I begin to be of that philosopher's opinion, who said, that whoever will entirely consult his own happiness must be little concerned about the happiness of others. Good nature is Quixotism, and every Princess Micomicona will lead her deliverer into a cage. (Henley ed., IX, 109-110)

48. In *An Essay on the Knowledge of the Characters of Men*, for example, Fielding carefully distinguished between good humor and good nature, which is

> ... that heavenly frame of soul, of which Jesus Christ Himself was the most perfect pattern; of which blessed person it is recorded, that He never was once seen to laugh, during His

whole abode on earth. And what indeed hath good-nature to do with a smiling countenance? . . . For . . . the world is so full of [the miseries and misfortunes of mankind], that scarce a day passes without inclining a truly good-natured man rather to tears than merriment. (Henley ed., XIV, 286)

49. Jensen ed., II, 1.
50. Jensen ed., II, 3.
51. Quoted in Richard P. Scowcroft's unpublished Ph.D. dissertation, "Anti-*Pamela*: The Problem of Retribution as it Affected Women in the Eighteenth Century Novel" (Harvard, 1946), p. 168. Scowcroft's sixth chapter, "Chastity," discusses the double standard in considerable detail.
52. Henley ed., XV, 244.
53. Jensen ed., I, 256.
54. Jensen ed., II, 115.
55. Henley ed., XII, 130-131.
56. *Amelia*, X, 2; Henley ed., VII, 193.
57. *Tom Jones*, XIV, 4; Henley ed., V, 108.
58. Henley ed., XV, 177, 178.
59. Henley ed., III, 209.
60. Cf. H. V. S. Ogden, "The Principles of Variety and Contrast in Seventeenth Century Aesthetics, and Milton's Poetry," *JHI*, X (1949), 159-182.
61. Dudden, I, 352. Several critics, of course, have made incidental attempts to justify the Wilson episode. In his recent monograph, John Butt briefly noticed one important function of the Wilson episode and its bearing on the novel as a whole: "Vanity of vanities is Mr. Wilson's theme." Since Fielding's action confines him to the highway, Professor Butt further observes, Wilson's story provides the opportunity to satirize the city. (*Fielding*, "Writers and Their Work," No. 57 [London, 1954], p. 18.) My own views of the function of the Wilson episode are in accord with Professor Butt's analysis, so far as it goes. The latest effort to explain the episodes in the novel is an article by I. B. Cauthen, Jr., "Fielding's Digressions in *Joseph Andrews*," *College English*, XVII (April, 1956), 379-382. Cauthen's observation that "these stories unmask the vices of hypocrisy and vanity in courtship, in marriage, and in the life of the rake" is, of course, true, but much too superficial.

Notes

62. Towers, "*Amelia* and the State of Matrimony," *RES*, New Series, V (1954), 145.

63. *The Covent-Garden Journal*, No. 57 (August 1, 1752); Jensen ed., II, 73.

64. Preface to the *Miscellanies*; Henley ed., XII, 247.

65. Henley ed., XII, 274.

66. Henley ed., XVI, 48.

67. Henley ed., XV, 218.

68. The similarities between the careers of Wilson and Tom Rakewell have been pointed out in some detail by Robert Etheridge Moore, *Hogarth's Literary Relationships* (Minneapolis, 1948), pp. 124-125.

69. *The Champion*, June 10, 1740; Henley ed., XV, 331.

70. The identification of the government lottery with Dame Fortune would have been familiar to Fielding's contemporaries. Appearing in *The Craftsman*, No. 804 (November 28, 1741), and reprinted in *The London Magazine*, for example, an attack on the Westminster Bridge lottery notices the practice of one "cunning Shaver, who obliges his Customers *gratis* with *exceeding beautiful Schemes of the Lottery, and a Copper-Plate Picture, representing* Fortune *throwing a* Bag of Gold *amongst the Adventurers, who buy Tickets at his Office.*" (*London Magazine*, X [December, 1741], 592.)

71. Henley ed., VI, 13-14. The following remarks in *The True Patriot*, No. 8 (December 24, 1745), anticipate the opening chapter of *Amelia*:

> As the great Cardinal *Richlieu* maintain'd, Fortune or blind Chance doth not interfere so much in the great Affairs of this World, as her complaisant Votaries the Fools would persuade us. What we call ill Luck, is generally ill Conduct. Generals and Ministers, who destroy their own Armies and Countries, and then lay the Blame on Fortune, talk as absurdly as the passionate bad Player at Chess, who swore he had lost the Game by one d——n'd unlucky Move, which exposed the King to Chequemate.

Compare Tom Jones: "But why do I blame Fortune? I am myself the cause of all my misery." (*Tom Jones*, XVIII, 2; Henley ed., V, 296.)

72. Digeon (p. 76) has noticed this.

73. Henley ed., V, 19.

A Study of *Joseph Andrews*

VII: Apology for the Clergy

1. Quoted by Work, *The Age of Johnson*, p. 147.
2. *Shamela*, Baker ed., p. 38.
3. See, for example, P. H. Ditchfield, *The Old-Time Parson* (London, 1908), pp. 100-112, and E. Hermitage Day, "The Country Clergy of the Restoration Period," *Theology*, XXXV (December, 1937), 354-360.
4. J. H. Overton, *Life in the English Church (1660-1714)* (London, 1885), p. 302.
5. From J. Churton Collins, ed., *An English Garner: Critical Essays and Literary Fragments* (New York, n. d.), I, 240.
6. South, Sermon LIX, "Christ's Promise, the Support of his despised Ministers," *Sermons*, III, 236.
7. Defoe, "Advice from the Scandal. Club," *Review*, No. 5 (March 13, 1705); in *Defoe's Review*, ed. Arthur Wellesley Secord, Facsimile Text Society (New York, 1938), II, 19-20.
8. Swift, *A Project for the Advancement of Religion, and the Reformation of Manners* (1709), in *The Prose Works of Jonathan Swift*, ed. Herbert Davis and others (Oxford, 1939), II, 54.
9. Secker, *The Charge of Thomas Lord Bishop of Oxford to the Clergy of his Diocese, in his Primary Visitation, 1738*, 2nd ed. (London, 1739), pp. 3-4. An important agent in the spread of the contempt of the clergy was the Restoration theatre, which Collier attacked in his *Short View of the Immorality and Prophaneness of the English Stage* (1698). In this respect, the following passage from Sir Richard Blackmore's Preface to *Prince Arthur* (1695) is especially pertinent:

> If a Clergy-man be introduc'd [in a play], as he often is, 'tis seldome for any other purpose but to abuse him, to expose his very *Character* and *Profession*: He must be a *Pimp*, a *Blockhead*, a *Hypocrite*; some *wretched Figure* he must make, and almost ever be so manag'd as to bring his very *Order* into *Contempt*. (Spingarn ed., III, 231)

10. In Collins, ed., I, 246.
11. *Ibid.*, I, 287.
12. *Ibid.*, I, 303.
13. *Ibid.*, I, 254.

Notes

14. *Ibid.*, I, 298.

15. Addison, *A Modest Plea for the Clergy; wherein Is Briefly considered, the Original, Antiquity, and necessary use of the Clergy, and the pretended and real Occasions of their Present Contempt* (London, 1709), in George Hickes, ed., *Three Short Treatises* (London, 1709), p. 4.

16. *Ibid.*, p. 104.

17. *Ibid.*, pp. 96, 100. Norman Sykes provides abundant evidence of these conditions and of the discrepancy between the living standards of the higher and lower clergy. See, especially, chs. IV and V ("The Ladder of Preferment" and "The Clerical Subalterns") in *Church and State in England in the XVIIIth Century* (Cambridge, 1934). Consult, too, A. Tindal Hart's informative book, *The Eighteenth Century Country Parson (Circa 1688-1830)* (Shrewsbury, 1955), ch. II, "The Beneficed and the Unbeneficed."

18. Hildrop, *The Contempt of the Clergy Considered in a Letter to a Friend*, in *The Miscellaneous Works of John Hildrop, D. D.* (London, 1754), II, 104.

19. Whitefield, Sermon X, "A Preservative against unsettled Notions, and want of Principles, in regard to Righteousness and Christian Perfection," *Works*, V, 155; and Sermon XXXVIII, "The Indwelling of the Spirit, the common Privilege of all Believers," *ibid.*, VI, 96.

20. Stackhouse, *The Miseries and Great Hardships of the Inferior Clergy*, 2nd ed. (London, n. d.), p. 107.

21. On the salary of a curate, Stackhouse remarks, "Thirty Pounds *per Annum* . . . is the common Run" (*ibid.*, p. 58). Sykes gives thirty to forty pounds as the average salary range for curates at this time. The most prosperous curates received sixty pounds per annum in the wealthy churches of London and Westminster, whereas the extreme of poverty was three or four pounds per year, reached in the dioceses of Carlisle and Wales (p. 206). Goldsmith's parson, we may remember, was "passing rich with forty pounds a year" (*The Deserted Village*, 1. 142).

22. Stackhouse, p. 12.

23. *Ibid.*, p. 17.

24. *Ibid.*, p. 35.

25. *Ibid.*, pp. 52-53.

26. *Ibid.*, pp. 55-56.

27. Hart, pp. 15-16.

28. Stackhouse, p. 70.
29. *Ibid.*, p. 60.
30. Henley ed., IX, 163.
31. *The Journal of a Voyage to Lisbon*, Henley ed., XVI, 306.
32. *Tom Jones*, XVIII, 4; Henley ed., V, 309.
33. *Tom Jones*, IV, 10, and VI, 9; Henley ed., III, 180, 309.
34. Henley ed., VII, 174-175.
35. *The True Patriot*, No. 14 (January 28-February 4, 1746).
36. *The Jacobite's Journal*, No. 32 (July 9, 1748).
37. *Tom Jones*, IV, 14; Henley ed., III, 201.
38. *Amelia*, VI, 3; Henley ed., VI, 285.
39. *The Jacobite's Journal*, No. 32 (July 9, 1748).
40. *The Champion* (April 19, 1740); Henley ed., XV, 283.
41. Henley ed., XV, 284-285.
42. Henley ed., XV, 287.
43. *Old England*, No. 266 (March 5, 1748).
44. *The Student, or The Oxford and Cambridge Monthly Miscellany* (Oxford, 1750-1751), II, 178.
45. *The Cry: A New Dramatic Fable* (London, 1754), III, 122-123.
46. In the third number of the "Apology," Fielding wrote: "Nay, so careful is the law, that the clergy should not be any ways hindered or disturbed in their spiritual office, that they are forbid to take any lands to farm or to buy and sell in markets, &c., under very severe penalties, that nothing might prevent them from discharging their duties to the souls of men." (*The Champion* [April 12, 1740]; Henley ed., XV, 278.)
47. One of Fielding's purposes in extensively revising *Joseph Andrews* was to sharpen the satire of his clergymen. Besides the fresh creation of the ignorant parson who so shamelessly misconstrues Adams' Aeschylus, other changes clarify the boorishness and hypocrisy of Trulliber and make the greed and vindictiveness of Adams' rector more vivid.
48. Barnabas, for example, offered to dedicate his sermons to a gentleman who, he hoped, would reward him with a good living. His offer was refused, however, and the living "given away in exchange for a Pointer" (I, 16). The merit of a man like Adams might well go a-begging under such conditions.

Notes

VIII: Conclusion

1. Henley ed., XV, 138.
2. Henley ed., XV, 259.

Index
of Authors, Subjects, and Titles

NOTE: References in italics are to quotations of works and authors. Additional subject references are included under the following separate entries: Fielding, *Joseph Andrews*, Barrow, Clarke, Hoadly, South, Tillotson, and Whitefield.

Abbey, Charles J., 162 (n. 29)
Abraham, 26, 28, 30-31, 32, 34-35, 36, 39, 41, 42-43, 89, 94, 104, 106, 109, 116, 129, 153-154, 180 (n.43.)
Abraham, 165 (n.30)
Absalom and Achitophel, 40
Addison, Joseph, *21-22*, 55, 133
Addison, Lancelot, 132, *133-134*
The Advancement and Reformation of Modern Poetry, 166 (n.34)
Advice to an Author, 12
Aeneid, 40, 89, 177 (n. 10)
Alexander, 36
Angliae Notitia, 131
Antinomianism, 14, 22-25, 81-84, 152, 162 (n.35)
"An Apology for the Censorious," *164 (n. 15)*
An Apology for the Life of Mr. Colley Cibber, 10
Apuleius, 119
Aristotle, 176 (n.7)
Arminianism, 15, 79
Articles of the Church, 15, 23
Augustine, St., 15, 152

Bacon, Francis, 40
Baker, Sheridan, 82, 176 (n.93)
Banerji, H. K., 157 (n.12)
Barrow, Isaac, x, 14, 21, 26, 28, 43, 53, 57, 71, 78, 79, 84, 89, 102, 106, 113, 152, 153, 159 (n.1), 161 (n.28), 165 (n.28), 168 (n.8)
Ideas: Abraham, 30-31, 34-35, 36; biblical heroes, 32-33, 34-37, 39, 89, 104, 106; charity, 18-19, 20, 100, 178 (n.26), 179 (nn.31-33); education, 16; examples and precepts, 32, 33-37, 39; good man (Christian hero), 27, 28, 30-33, 34-37, 163 (n.1); good nature, 16-17, 57, 71-72, 171 (n.32); Hobbes, 19; journey allegory, 41-42, 166 (n.37); Joseph, 31-32, 34-35; prosperity and adversity, 49-51; self-love (vanity), 19-20, 45, 53; Stoicism, 15.
Works: "The Being of God Proved from the Frame of Human Nature," *16*; "The Consideration of Our Latter End," *45, 167 (n.6)*; "The Duty and Reward of Bounty to the Poor," *17, 18-19, 27, 30, 49-50, 100*, 159 (n.1), *179 (nn.31-33)*; "Keep thy Heart with All Diligence," *15*; "Of Being Imitators of Christ," *26, 28, 32-39, 43, 89, 102, 104, 106, 113*; "Of Contentment," *41-*

188

Index

42, 50-51; "Of Self-Confidence, &c.," 16, 17, 19; "Of Self-Love in General," 19-20; "Of the Love of Our Neighbour," 28, 31, 171 (n.32), 178 (n.26); "Of the Virtue and Reasonableness of Faith," 31-32, 166 (n.37); "Of Walking as Christ Did," 28; "The Pleasantness of Religion," 20; "The Profitableness of Godliness," 47, 168 (n.8); "The Reward of Honouring God," 163 (n.1).
biblical epic, 39-41, 89, 113, 164 (n.15), 165 (nn.30,32)
Blackmore, Sir Richard, 41, 165 (n.28), 184 (n.9)
Bloom, Edward A., 177 (n.8)
Boethius, 45, 49, 124, 126
Boileau (Despréaux), Nicolas, 41, 166 (n.32)
Branch, Mary E., 158 (n.14)
Bunyan, John, 41, 89, 91
Burnet, Gilbert, 164 (n.16)
Butt, John, 182 (n.61)

Calvin, John, 15
Calvinism, 14-15, 22-24, 55-56, 61
Canning, Elizabeth, 57
Cato, 46
Cauthen, I. B., Jr., 182 (n.61)
Cervantes Saavedra, Miguel de, 3, 9, 85-86, 89, 119
Chamberlayne, Edward, 131
Characteristics, 12-13
The Charge . . . to the Clergy of his Diocese (Secker), 131-132
charity, x, 14-22, 26, 27, 30, 48, 54, 61, 66-72, 75-81, 84, 88, 152, 153, 160 (n.11), 175 (n.86), 178 (n.26), 179 (nn.31-33)
chastity, 26, 30, 32, 88, 89, 93, 113-118, 153, 182 (n.51)
Chillingworth, William, 109
Christian epic (see biblical epic)
The Christian Hero, 28
Cibber, Colley, 4, 6, 10
Cicero, 11, 13, 24, 45, 46
Clarke, Samuel, x, 14, 28, 79, 152, 159 (n.1), 171 (n.32)
  Ideas: Abraham, 31, 42-43, 104; charity, 17, 20-21, 160 (n.11); deism, 17; education, 17; good man (Christian hero), 27, 28, 31, 42-43, 104, 163 (n.8); good nature, 16-17, 171 (n.32); journey allegory, 42-43; Providence, 49; prosperity and adversity, 50.
  Works: "The Character of a Good Man," 28, 31, 42-43, 104; "The End of God's Afflicting Men," 50; "The Excellency of Moral Qualifications," 27, 163 (n.8); "How to Judge of Moral Actions," 17; "Of a Future Judgment," 20-21; "Of Believing in God," 28, 31; "Of Future Rewards and Punishments," 160 (n.11); "Of the Duty of Charity," 17, 160 (n.11); "Of the Nature of Moral and Positive Duties," 160 (n.11); "Of the Virtue of Charity," 160 (n.11); "The Shortness and Vanity of Humane Life," 168 (n.16); "That Every Man Shall Finally Receive According to His Works," 49.
classical ideal, 45-48, 88-89, 90-94
clergy, 130-136, 153, 184 (n.9), 185 (nn.17,21)
Coleridge, Samuel T., x, 87
Coley, William B., xi
Collier, Jane, 175 (n.82)
Collier, Jeremy, 184 (n.9)
Collier, Margaret, 175 (n.82)
Congleton, J. E., 47
Congreve, William, 161 (n.28)
The Conscious Lovers, x
Consolation of Philosophy, 49, 124
The Contempt of the Clergy Considered, 132, 134
Correspondence (Richardson), 4, 156 (n.6)
Cowley, Abraham, 39-40, 47
Cradock, Charlotte (Mrs. Henry Fielding), 121, 151
The Craftsman, 183 (n.70)
Crane, R. S., 12, 70-71
Cross, Wilbur, 12, 164 (n.16), 175 (n.82)
The Cry, 142-143

189

A Study of *Joseph Andrews*

Dante Alighieri, 91
David, 39
Davideis (Cowley), 39
Davideis (Ellwood), 40
David Simple, 86-87
Davis, J. L., 9, 157 (n.10)
Day, E. Hermitage, 184 (n.3)
de Castro, J. Paul, 157 (n.12)
Defoe, Daniel, 131
deism, 11, 12-13, 17, 24, 48
Dennis, John, 41, 165 (n.28)
The Deserted Village, 185 *(n.21)*
Desmarets de Saint-Sorlin, Jean, 39, 165 (n.30)
Dickens, Charles, 154
Digeon, Aurélien, 11, 87, 157 (nn. 8,12), 183 (n.72)
A Discourse Concerning the Original and Progress of Satire, 166 (n.34)
Ditchfield, P. H., 184 (n.3)
Dolce, Lodovico, 165 (n.30)
Donne, John, 10
Don Quixote, 43, 85-86, 88, 111, 142, 176 (n.1), 181 (n.47)
Downs, Brian W., 157 (n.12)
Dryden, John, 40-41, 47, 165 (nn. 28,32)
Dudden, F. Homes, *86, 119,* 158 (n.12)
Dyer, John, 47

Eachard, John, *132-133*
Ecclesiastes, 45, 49, 120
education, 16-17, 59-60, 62-63, 84, 93-94, 152
Elegy in a Country Churchyard, 45
Ellwood, Thomas, 40
Essay on Charity, 56
An Essay on the Freedom of Wit and Humour, 12, 158 (n.22)
Esther, 40

Familiar Letters between the Principal Characters in David Simple, 121
The Female Quixote, 86
Fénelon, François de Salignac de la Mothe, 85, 89

Fielding, Charlotte (daughter), 151
Fielding, Henry
 Ideas: Barrow, 14, 32, 79, 89, 152, 159 (n.1); Calvinism, 55-56, 57, 61, 169 (n.6); charity, x, 54, 61, 66-72, 75-81, 84, 88, 139, 174 (n.74), 175 (nn.82,86), 179 (nn.27,31); chastity, 88, 89, 113-118, 164 (n.15); Clarke, 14, 79, 152, 159 (n.1); classical ideal, 88-89, 91-93, 177 (n.19), 178 (n.22); clergy, 78, 89, 105-106, 130, 136-142, 148-149, 153, 156 (n.5), 180 (n.42); education, 59-60, 62-63, 84, 110, 123, 171 (n.34); free will and determinism, 57-59, 60-62, 64, 84, 175 (n.86), 183 (n.71); good nature, x, 54-63, 65-81, 84, 89, 170 (n.15), 172 (nn.48,49), 173 (nn. 56, 60, 62), 174 (n.72), 181 (nn.45,47,48); Hoadly, 14, 20, 79, 95-98, 152, 159 (n.1); Hobbes, etc., 55-56, 57, 169 (nn.6,9); Joseph, 32, 116, 164 (n.15); judgment, 55, 72-75, 84, 174 (n.67); marriage, 120-121; Milton and the Christian epic, 40, 90, 165 (n.32); *Pamela*, 4-11, 63, 113, 156 (nn.5,6); passions, 57-60, 61, 64, 84; Shaftesbury and deism, 11, 12-13, 62-63, 158 (n.22), 170 (n.32); South, 22, 161 (n.28); Stoicism, 11-12, 13, 66-68, 158 (n.18); Tillotson, 14, 64, 79, 152, 159 (n.1); vanity (self-love), 19, 43, 52-53, 88-89, 110, 112-113, 169 (n.9); Whitefield and Methodism, 25, 61, 78, 81-84, 176 (n.93), 180 (n.42).
 Works: *Amelia*, 11, 16, 49, 56, *59-60,* 61, *62,* 63, *64, 67, 68, 73, 76, 81, 83,* 89, *93,* 106, 108, 110, 114, *116,* 120, 123, *127,* 130, 137, *138, 140,* 150-151, 159 (n.1), *164 (n.15),* 168 (n. 11), *169 (n.9), 170 (n.15), 171 (n.34), 173 (n.62),* 177 (n.10), *179 (n.27), 181 (n.45),* 183 (n.

190

Index

71); *The Champion,* 4, 10, 13, 14, 52, 55, 57-58, 59, 61, 62, 63-64, 69, 72, 74, 75, 76-77, 81, 93, 98, 101, *105-106,* 110, 111, 114, *116-117,* 118, *121-122,* 130, 131, *140-142, 150, 152, 158 (nn. 14,22),* 159 (n.1), 161 (n.28), 162 (n.29), 173 (n.61), *174 (n. 74), 180 (n.42), 186 (n.46);* A *Charge to the Grand Jury,* 91; *A Clear State of the Case of Elizabeth Canning,* 57; *The Coffee-House Politician, 181 (n.47); The Covent-Garden Journal,* 60, *61-62, 63, 67-68, 71-72, 73, 76, 77-78, 80-81, 86,* 90, *92,* 99, 101, *112-113,* 115, *120,* 123, *159 (n.1), 161 (n.28), 165 (n.32), 173 (n.56),* 175 (n.82); *The Covent-Garden Tragedy,* 8; *David Simple* (Preface), *86-87*; "A Description of U—n G—(Alias New Hog's Norton)," *170 (n.16); Don Quixote in England, 174 (n.72); An Essay on Conversation,* 60; *An Essay on the Knowledge of the Characters of Men, 58-59, 66,* 72, *76, 101,* 179 (n.31), *181 (n.48); Examples of the Interposition of Providence, 171 (n. 32),* 175 (n.82); *Familiar Letters, 121, 171 (n.32); The Fathers,* 72, *74, 172 (n.48); An Inquiry into the Causes of the Late Increase of Robbers,* 60, *69-70,* 73, *75; The Jacobite's Journal, 62, 136, 139, 140,* 173 (n.61); *Jonathan Wild,* 72, *81,* 102, *120,* 137, 169 (n.6), *172 (n.49),* 173 *(n.60), 178 (n.22); Joseph Andrews* (see separate entry); *The Journal of a Voyage to Lisbon, 60-61, 137; A Journey from this World to the Next,* 58, *79-80,* 114, 137, 165 (n.32), *175 (n. 86); Juvenal's Sixth Satire Modernised,* 8; Letter to Lyttelton, *70-71; The Letter Writers,* 91, 137; *Love in Several Masques, 91; Miscellanies* (Preface), 79,

102, *121,* 169 *(n.6); Miss Lucy in Town,* 92; *The Modern Husband,* 115; "Of Good-Nature," *65-66; Of the Remedy of Affliction,* 12, *158 (n.18); Of True Greatness,* 91, 159 (n.1); *A Proposal for Making an Effectual Provision for the Poor,* 64; *Shamela,* 4, 5-6, 8-10, *130,* 151, *156 (nn.5,6),* 158 (n.14), 162 (n.29), 176 (n.93); "To a Friend on the Choice of a Wife," *120-121;* "To John Hayes, Esq.," *58; Tom Jones,* x, *11, 13, 37-38, 48, 55-56, 59,* 60, *63,* 65, 68, 69, *70,* 71, 72, *74-75, 76, 78-79, 81, 82-83, 90, 92,* 100, 111, 114, *116, 119,* 120, *129, 137, 139,* 150, *154, 159 (n.1),* 165 (n.32), *172* (n.38), *173 (n.62),* 176 (n.7), *177 (n.19), 183 (n. 71); Tom Thumb,* 8; *The True Patriot,* 74, *99, 100, 123-124, 139, 169 (n.6),* 178 (n.24), *183 (n.71); A True State of the Case of Bosavern Penlez, 174 (n.67); The Vernoniad,* 8, 165 (n.32); *The Wedding-Day, 115-116.*
Fielding, Mrs. Henry (see Cradock)
Fielding, Sarah, 86, *113,* 121, *142-143,* 175 (n.82)
Fortune and Providence, 45, 48-51, 183 (n.70)
Fracastorius, Hieronymus, 165 (n. 30)

The Gentleman's Magazine, 4, 29, 47, *163 (n.6),* 164 (n.15), 167 (n.4)
Georgic (Second), 46, 120
Gideon, 40
Gil Blas, 85, 88
Godeau, Antoine, 39
Goldsmith, Oliver, 47, *185 (n.21)*
good man (Christian hero), 26-51, 54, 89, 116, 163 (nn.5,6)
good nature, x, 12, 14-19, 27, 54-63, 65-81, 84, 89, 152
Gray, Thomas, 45
The Gray's-Inn Journal, 179 (n.34)
Green, Matthew, 47

The Grounds and Occasions of the Contempt of the Clergy, 132-133
The Grounds of Criticism in Poetry, 166 (n.34)
The Guardian, 131, 167 (n.5)

Haller, William, *166 (n.36)*
Hart, A. Tindal, 185 (n.17)
Havens, Raymond D., 167 (n.4)
Hawkins, Sir John, *12*
Henley, John, 40
Herbert, Edward, first Baron of Cherbury, 21
Hildrop, John, 132, *134*, 135
Hill, Aaron, *4*, 40
The History of My Own Times, 164 (n.16)
The History of Ophelia, 113
Hoadly, Benjamin, x, 14, 23, 28, 79, 96, 109, 152, 153, 159 (n.1), 163 (n.8)
    Ideas: charity, 17-18, 20, 22, 30, 95, 178 (n.26); chastity, 30; eucharist, 20, 96, 97-98, 109; good man (Christian hero), 28, 30; Good Samaritan, 95, 178 (n.26); journey allegory, 42; retirement, 48.
    Works: "The Different Characters of John the Baptist, and Jesus Christ," *48*; "The Good Samaritan," *18*, 22, 28, *95*, 97, *178 (n.26)*; "The Nature of the Kingdom, or Church, of Christ," 20, *30*; "No Continuing City Here, &c.," *42*; "Of the Divisions, and Cruelties, Falsely Imputed to Christianity," *17-18*; *A Plain Account of the Nature and End of the Sacrament,* 20, 96, *97*, 98, 159 (n.1); "St. Paul's Discourse to Felix," 28
Hobbes, Thomas, 14-15, 19, 53, 55-56, 71, 98, 124, 179 (n.35)
Hogarth, William, ix, 23, 122-123, 183 (n.68)
Homer, 40, 85, 118
Horace, ix, 45, 46, 176 (n.7)
Horae Lyricae, 166 (n.34)
Hughes, Leo, *6*

Hume, David, 57

Iliad, 40, 87
Irwin, W. R., *54*

James, St., *18*, 30, 104
Job, 45, 49, 126
Joesten, Maria, *11*, 66
John the Baptist, 48
Johnson, Samuel, 23, 45, 47
Jonathan, 39
Joseph, 26, 30, 31-32, 34-35, 39, 41, 89, 106, 113, 116, 129, 153-154, 164 (n.15)
Joseph (Fracastorius), 165 (n.30)
Joseph (Morillon), 165 (n.30)
Joseph (Saint-Amant), 165 (n.30)
Joseph Andrews
    Ideas: Abraham, 34-35, 89, 94, 104, 106, 109, 116, 129, 153-154, 180 (n.43); allegory, 88-89, 90-94, 118, 120, 129, 154; Barrow, 26, 32-39, 43, 89, 100, 102, 104, 106, 113, 153, 159 (n.1), 179 (n.32); biblical epic, 39-41, 89, 104, 113, 153-154, 177 (n.10); burlesque, 6-11, 157 (nn.8-10), 158 (n.22); charity, 54, 88, 94-97, 98-104, 106, 111, 116, 120, 125, 126, 128, 153, 178 (n.27); chastity, 32, 88, 89, 93, 104, 106, 111, 113-118, 153; classical ideal, 45-48, 88-89, 90-94, 120-122, 123, 127-129, 154, 177 (n.9); clergy, x, 89, 96, 104-110, 130, 135, 136, 140, 142-149, 153, 180 (n.44), 186 (nn.47-48); deism, 13, 48, 124-125; education, 33, 93-94, 106-107, 110, 120, 123-124, 129, 169 (n.14), 170 (n.19); Fortune, 45, 48-51, 124-127; good man (Christian hero), 33, 38, 54, 65, 89, 102-110, 116, 129, 153-154; good nature, 54, 65, 89, 98-99, 100, 102, 110-113; Hoadly, 20, 95-96, 97-98, 109, 159 (n.1); Hobbes, etc., 98-99, 124; Joseph, 32, 34-35, 89, 93, 106, 113, 116, 118, 129, 153-154, 164 (n.15); literary parallels, 85-86, 104, 111,

Index

176 (n.1), 181 (n.47); marriage, 91, 92-93, 120-121, 127-129, 154; *Pamela*, 3, 5-11, 113, 117, 151, 152, 157 (nn.8,10,12); Ridiculous, ix, 6-7, 10, 52, 63, 103-104, 110, 112-113, 123, 151-152, 179 (n.35); Stoicism, 12, 67, 109; Tillotson, 159 (n.1); unity, x, 3, 9, 86-88, 118-119, 129, 153; vanity (self-love), 19, 43, 45-48, 52-53, 88-89, 91-94, 98-99, 103-104, 112-113, 119-122, 123, 125, 127-128, 129, 152, 153-154, 182 (n.61); Whitefield, 25, 96-97, 98, 100, 107-108, 144, 152; Wilson episode, 3, 13, 19, 44-51, 91, 93, 94, 102, 113, 118-129, 154, 182 (n.61), 183 (n.68).
Juvenal, 34, 45, 46, 47, 120

Kettle, Arnold, 157 (n.8)
King James Bible, 109
Kitchin, George, 157 (n.10)

The Last Judgment of Men and Angels, 40
Leake, James, 156 (n.6)
Le Bossu, René, 88, 165 (n.28), 176 (n.7)
Lennox, Charlotte, 86
Le Sage, Alain René, 85, 89, 119
Leviathan, 15
Licensing Act of 1737, 151
The Life of Our Blessed Lord and Saviour, 40
Lillo, George, 163 (n.6)
Locke, John, 23, 74
The London Magazine, 10, 159 (n.1), 164 (n.15), 183 (n.70)
Longinus, 176 (n.7)
Lucian, 79
Lucretius, 45, 46
Lyttelton, George, 70, 175 (n.82)

Macaulay, Thomas B., 130
Mack, Maynard, 54, 177 (n.9)
McKillop, Allan D., 156 (n.1)
Mandeville, Bernard de, 19, 53, 55-56, 98-99
Marianne, 85

Marivaux, Pierre Carlet de Chamblain de, 85
Marriage Act of 1753, 109
Martial, 45, 46
Meredith, George, *179 (n.35)*
Methodism, 6, 22-25, 78, 81-84, 96-97, 98, 152, 161 (n.29), 162 (n.35), 176 (n.93), 180 (n.42)
Middleton, Conyers, 6
Millar, Andrew, 159 (n.1)
Milton, John, *40*, 45, 90, 165 (n.32)
The Miseries and Great Hardships of the Inferior Clergy, 135-136
A Modest Plea for the Clergy, 132, 133-134
Moore, Robert E., 183 (n.68)
The Moralists, 47
Morillon, Julien-Gatien, 165 (n.30)
Moses, 39
Murphy, Arthur, 79, 103
Murry, J. Middleton, xi

Newcomb, Thomas, 40
Noah, 39

Odyssey, 40, 85, 87
Ogden, H. V. S., 182 (n.60)
Old England, 142
Oldham, John, 47
"On Joseph and Potiphar's Wife," 164 (n.15)
Overton, John H., *130*, 162 (n.29)
Ovid, 45, 46

Pamela, 3-6, 8-11, 43, 63, 85, 113, 117, 151, 152, 156 (nn.1,5,6), 164 (n.15)
Paradise Lost, *40*, 90, 165 (n.32)
Paradise Regained, 40
A Paraphrase upon the Psalms of David, 166 (n.34)
Parnell, Thomas, 47
passions, 57-60, 61, 64, 84
Paul, St., 18, 75, 78
Le Paysan parvenu, 85
The Pearl, 175 (n.86)
Peirce, 175 (n.82)
Pelagianism, 14-15, 21, 23, 60, 62, 79, 80, 84, 152, 161 (n.28), 175 (n.86)

Pelagius, 152
Pelagius, Porcupinus (pseud.), 142
Penlez, Bosavern, 174 (n.67)
The Pilgrim's Progress, 41
Poems (Cowley), 39-40
Pope, Alexander, 4, 47, 58, 156 (n.6)
Powers, Lyall H., 177 (n.10)
Prae-existence, 40
Prince Arthur, 166 (n.34), 184 (n.9)
Prior, Matthew, 40, 45, 47
A Project for the Advancement of Religion, 131
Psalms, 45

Quintilian, 63

The Rake's Progress, 122
Rapin, René, 47
Redman, 175 (n.82)
Reed, Amy, 45, 167 (n.4)
Review (Defoe), 131
Richardson, Samuel, 4, 5-6, 8-11, 37, 63, 85, 150, 151, 156 (n.6), 157 (n.9)
La Rochefoucauld, François VI de, 55, 169 (n.9)
Le Roman comique, 85, 88
Røstvig, Maren-Sofie, 167 (n.4)

Saint-Amant, M.-A. Girard, Sieur de, 39, 165 (n.30)
Saint-Peres, Sieur de, 165 (n.30)
Samson, 39
Samson Agonistes, 40
Sayce, R. A., 39, 165 (n.30)
Scanderbeg, 163 (n.6)
Scarron, Paul, 85, 89
Scowcroft, Richard P., 182 (n.51)
Secker, Thomas, 131-132
Seneca, 24, 45, 46
Shaftesbury, Anthony Ashley Cooper, third earl of, 11, 12-13, 17, 47, 62-63, 69, 158 (n.22), 170 (n.32)
Shepperson, Archibald B., 157 (n.10)
Sherburn, George, x, xi, 56-57, 87-88, 91, 177 (n.10)

A Short View of the Immorality and Prophaneness of the English Stage, 184 (n.9)
Slocock, Benjamin, 4
Smollett, Tobias, 23
Socinianism, 15
Solomon on the Vanity of the World, 40, 45
South, Robert, 22, 32, 161 (n.28), 167 (n.7), 171(n.32)
  Ideas: Antinomianism, 22; clergy, 131; Joseph, 32; prosperity and adversity, 168 (nn.12,15); Providence, 49; retirement, 47-48.
  Works: "All Contingencies under the Direction of God's Providence," 49; "Christ's Promise, the Support of his despised Ministers," 131; "Covetousness an Absurdity in Reason and a Contradiction to Religion," 47; "Deliverance from Temptation the Privilege of the Righteous," 32; "The Nature, Causes, and Consequences of Envy," 47-48; "The Practice of Religion Enforced by Reason," 167 (n.7); "Prosperity Ever Dangerous to Virtue," 168 (nn.12,15).
The Spectator, 21-22, 28-29, 163 (n.5)
Spenser, Edmund, 91
Stackhouse, Thomas, 135-136, 146, 185 (n.21)
Steele, Richard, x, 28-29, 102, 131
Sterne, Laurence, 55
Stoicism, 11-12, 13, 14-15, 28, 66-68, 158 (n.18), 168 (n.8)
Stromberg, Roland N., 15
The Student, 142
Swann, George R., 12, 57
Swedenberg, H. T., 41, 165 (n.28), 166 (n.32), 177 (n.8)
Swift, Jonathan, 131
Sykes, Norman, 185 (nn.17,21)

The Tatler, 131
Taylor, Dick, Jr., 177 (n.13)
Télémaque, 85

Index

Thackeray, William M., 154
Third Satire (Juvenal), 46, 47, 120
Thomson, James, 47
Thornbury, Ethel M., 159 (n.1), 166 (n.32)
Tillotson, John, x, 14, 24, 28, 31, 64, 79, 152, 153, 159 (n.1), 161 (n.28), 163 (n.8), 171 (n.32)
  Ideas: Abraham, 31, 43; Antinomianism, 22; charity, 19-21, 30; chastity, 30, 116; education, 16; good man (Christian hero), 28, 30, 31, 43; good nature, 15, 16, 171 (n.32); Hobbes, 15, 19; journey allegory, 43; Stoicism, 15.
  Works: "The Advantage of Religion to Society," 64; "The Condition of the Gospel-Covenant, and the Merit of Christ, Consistent," 21; "The Difficulties of a Christian Life Consider'd," 16; "The Example of Jesus in Doing Good," 20, 28; "Good Men Strangers and Sojourners upon Earth," 28, 31, 43; "Of Doing All to the Glory of God," 19; "Of Forgiveness of Injuries, and Against Revenge," 15; "Of the Form, and the Power of Godliness," 20; "Of the Necessity of Good Works," 19, 22; "Of the Work Assign'd to Every Man, and the Season for Doing It," 30, 116; "The True Remedy Against the Troubles of Life," 15.
Tillyard, E. M. W., 41, 166 (n.36)
Tindal, Matthew, 23
Tonson, Jacob III, 159 (n.1)
Towers, A. R., 120, 159 (n.1), 168 (n.11)
Traité du poëme epique, 88, 165 (n.28)
Trapp, Joseph, 81, 162 (n.29), 180 (n.42)

vanity (self-love), 19-20, 27-28, 43, 45-48, 52-53, 63, 88-89, 91-94, 112-113

The Vanity of Human Wishes, 45
La Vie de Joseph, 165 (n.30)
Virgil, 40, 45, 46, 120, 165 (n.32)
La Vita di Giuseppe, 165 (n.30)

Wallace, Robert M., 164 (n.17)
Walpole, Sir Robert, 5
Warburton, William, 175 (n.82)
Warton, Joseph, 47
Watt, I. P., 164 (n.16), 177 (n.10)
Watts, Isaac, 41
Wesley, John, 22
Wesley, Samuel, 40
Whitefield, George, 6, 22, 61, 81-84, 96-97, 100, 107-108, 144, 152, 153, 158 (n.14), 176 (n.93), 180 (n.42)
  Ideas: enthusiasm, 23, 83, 153, 162 (n.20); justification by faith, 23-25, 82-83, 162 (n.35); reformation of Church, 96, 107-108, 135, 144, 153.
  Works: "The Folly and Danger of Being Not Righteous Enough," 24, 25, 162 (nn.29,35); "The Indwelling of the Spirit, the Common Privilege of All Believers," 24, 135; "A Letter to the Religious Societies of England," 23-24; "Marks of a True Conversion," 24; "A Preservative against unsettled Notions, and want of Principles, in regard to Righteousness and Christian Perfection," 135; A Short Account of God's Dealings with the Reverened Mr. George Whitefield, 82; "What Think Ye of Christ?," 23
The Whole Duty of Man, 24
Willey, Basil, 40
Wilson, 174 (n.67)
Woodford, Samuel, 40
Woods, Charles B., 157 (n.8), 158 (n.14)
Work, James A., x, xi, xii, 11, 158 (n.14), 184 (n.1)

Y. Y., 164 (n.16)
Yost, Calvin D., 167 (n.4)